**Bible Study Series**

# Isaiah

## Prophet of Deliverance and Messianic Hope
### Part 1

*Linda Shaw*

*Helen Silvey*

*Jeannie McCullough, Executive Editor*

**BEACON HILL PRESS**

OF KANSAS CITY

KANSAS CITY, MISSOURI

ISBN 083-412-0291

Printed in the
United States of America

Cover Design: Darlene Filley

**Library of Congress Cataloging-in-Publication Data**

Shaw, Linda, 1951-
   Isaiah : prophet of deliverance and messianic hope / Linda Shaw, Helen Silvey ; Jeannie McCullough, executive editor.
     p. cm.—(Wisdom of the Word Bible study series ; 1)
   Includes bibliographical references.
   ISBN 0-8341-2029-1 (pbk.)
   1. Bible. O.T. Isaiah—Textbooks. I. Silvey, Helen, 1931- II. Title. III. Series.
   BS1515.55 .S43 2003
   224'.1'0071—dc21

2002013154

10  9  8  7  6  5  4  3  2  1

# Contents

# About Wisdom of the Word

**Wisdom of the Word** (W.O.W.) was founded in 1986 by Jeannie McCullough in Bethany, Oklahoma. It began as a weekly Bible study at Bethany First Church of the Nazarene. In the first year the study grew to over 400 members, and women from other churches and the community began joining. The local enrollment of Wisdom of the Word eventually exceeded 1,000 and has included men, women, and children of all ages and many denominations. Wisdom of the Word has been an instrument in uniting the community of believers as well as reaching the unchurched and the lost. It is now ministering to thousands through videos and cassette tapes and other programs such as Children of the Word, prison ministries, and missions.

## About the Name

W.O.W. began as "Women of the Word." Then when men began to join in the study with the women, the name was changed to Wisdom of the Word, not only to retain the W.O.W. acronym but also to reflect the mission:

> To have our lives visibly changed by gaining wisdom from God's Word and responding in radical obedience to His voice.

## About Jeannie McCullough

Jeannie McCullough is a pastor's wife, mother, and grandmother. Her life and ministry have taken her to Bethany, Oklahoma, where her husband, Mel, is the senior pastor at Bethany First Church of the Nazarene. She understands firsthand how radical obedience to God's Word can change a life.

Southern Nazarene University granted Jeannie an honorary doctorate in 1997. Due to her humor and honesty as well as her unique insights and application of the Scriptures in daily living, she is in great demand as a speaker throughout North America. Jeannie strives to be a "salt tablet" who will make others thirsty for God's Word. As she has committed herself to being a student of the Word, God has given her many opportunities to share what He is teaching her.

## About the Authors

● LINDA SHAW is a licensed clinical social worker and began the W.O.W. prison ministry at a women's prison in the Oklahoma City area. She has three children: Jonathan, Jenny, and Daniel.

● HELEN SILVEY has been a group leader for W.O.W. for many years and is very active in Bethany First Church of the Nazarene. She is a widow with four grown children.

## Interested in starting a W.O.W. Bible study?

If you are interested in starting a W.O.W. Bible study, attending a study in your area, or ordering additional materials, please contact the W.O.W. outreach office in Bethany, Oklahoma, at 405-491-6274.

# Introduction to Isaiah

Isaiah predicted, portrayed, and proclaimed God's message. He predicted events in the near future and distant future. He portrayed the people's sin yet also their coming Savior. He proclaimed the day of the Lord, meaning God would not be patient with Judah's disobedience forever—a time of judgment would come. These predictions, portrayals, and proclamations were the theme of Isaiah's message.

*In the year that King Uzziah died* (Isaiah 6:1) was probably 739 B.C. This is the time when God called and commissioned Isaiah to speak to His people of Judah regarding their sin and about salvation and the Savior, the Messiah. Thus, the prophetic portion of the Bible begins with the Book of Isaiah. These 16 prophetic books of the Old Testament had a predictive element but were also the voice for God when the king or priests or people were not speaking for Him.

The "making of a prophet" involves six steps, according to *Beacon Bible Commentary*.[1] Step one is a social crisis. Then comes the heavenly vision. Third comes the humble confession. A personal cleansing is step four, followed by a call to service, and finally is the irrevocable commitment.

A prophet had to qualify for his job through accuracy. According to God's Word, *You may say to yourselves, "How can we know when a message has not been spoken by the LORD?" If what a prophet proclaims in the name of the LORD does not take place or come true, that is a message the LORD has not spoken. That prophet has spoken presumptuously. Do not be afraid of him* (Deuteronomy 18:21-22). Isaiah advised "bewareness" of false prophets.

Isaiah predicted the first and second comings of Christ. The Bible contains 300 prophecies of the first coming of Christ that were literally fulfilled. Many of Isaiah's prophecies regarding the Second Coming are followed up in the Book of Revelation. His predictions were not all gloom and doom, for he saw the day of the Lord and His glory.

Isaiah belonged to his own time and culture but was not limited by it. At the young age of 20 he began this mighty message and continued it for 50 years. He provides a subject of analogy to late cartoonist and philosopher Charles Schultz. For nearly 50 years he shared Charlie Brown and friends in the *Peanuts* comic strip series published in newspapers throughout North America. Schultz began the fulfillment of his childhood dream at age 27 and died on the very day his last comic strip installment appeared in newspapers. This man and his loved characters became such an intricate part of the life of our culture that it seemed they would never end.

The same surely could have been said of Isaiah in his day. His words today still hold some prediction. His portrayal of Christ is never-changing. His proclamations regarding sin remain the same.

Isaiah gives us very little history of himself or projection of his personality. He was probably from a family of rank, for he seemed to have access to the king and high priest. He married a woman the Bible refers to as *the prophetess* (Isaiah 8:3) and fathered two sons, Shear-jashub, meaning "a remnant shall return," and Maher-shalal-hash-baz, meaning "hurrying to the prey." He was a contemporary of Amos and Hosea, who were prophesying in the Northern Kingdom while Isaiah was in the South.

---

*As you begin each day, use this acrostic to help you study:*

**W**ait *for the Holy Spirit to teach you as you read His Word.*

**O**bey *what God instructs you to do.*

**R**emember *to praise God for insights and promises fulfilled.*

**D**iscover *for yourself the incredible faithfulness of God!*

When Isaiah received his call from God, the nation of Israel, which was the Northern Kingdom, had already fallen to Assyria. God's promises to Israel had been that they would always have their nation and a king as long as they obeyed His Law. But after many warnings and disasters, the people still did not take this seriously and lost control of their country. When this occurred in the North, the South was separate—since through its own internal fighting, Israel had been divided into a northern and southern kingdom. Judah was threatened at this time by Assyria also and was looking to Egypt for help. Uzziah and Hezekiah were servants of God and were enlightened rulers. The nation was maintained while they were on the throne, but during the years of Ahaz fear was ever present, for he was not a godly man and disobeyed the laws of God.

As a young man, Isaiah must have witnessed the rapid development of Judah into a military and commercial state of some strength. Under Uzziah the country experienced prosperity and might that they had not seen since the days of Solomon. They had walled cities and tower fortresses, along with a large army. Wars were won with Philistia and Arabia, and tribute was being paid by the Ammonites. Commerce thrived on the seaport on the Red Sea.

During Isaiah's 50 years, Jotham, Ahaz, and Hezekiah were the kings. Egypt was a power to the south and Assyria the threat to the north. Isaiah prophesied regarding the various invasions by Assyria: the first time was in 734-732 B.C. by Tiglath-pileser III, when Ahaz was king; the second in 725-720 B.C. by Shalmaneser IV and Sargon; the third in 721 B.C., when Samaria fell; the fourth in 712-710 B.C., with Sargon again leading the invasion; and the fifth in 701 B.C., when Sennacherib headed the army and threatened Israel.

Socially, Judah had become classes of the rich and poor. The city government was corrupt, and judges could be bribed. For the rich there was luxury and idleness and a lack of concern for those less fortunate.

Religiously, there were superstitions from the East and the worship of Moloch. Baalism was common, along with the show of religion with no substance to it. Religion had separated from how one lived daily life.

Isaiah was a political and religious counselor in Judah, in addition to being a poet and orator. His beauty of expression is unsurpassed in the Bible. He was always looking to the future and cried for national righteousness.

God called this prophet: *Then I heard the voice of the Lord saying, "Whom shall I send? And who will go for us?"* (6:8). Isaiah dared to answer the call saying, *Here am*

*I. Send me!* (verse 8). God then commissioned him and gave him a message, saying, *Go and tell this people* (verse 9). That commission lasted 50 years until, according to legend, Manasseh had him sawed in two. But Isaiah brought that call to completion. He never compromised his commission or message. He was faithful from start to finish.

Isaiah learned, suffered, and matured as a man during his 50 years of prophecy. His theme was salvation by faith. He believed true worship is a "God moment," in which the Most High has been contacted. Quietness leads to insight, true communion, and a change in heart and outward behavior. Ritualism is meaningless without true worship. A vision of God brings awareness of our sinfulness and unworthiness.

In the New Testament are 66 direct quotes from Isaiah. Some have called his writings "the fifth Gospel." Twenty of the 27 books of the New Testament have quotes from Isaiah woven into their fabric. The Bible itself has 66 books— 39 in the Old Testament and 27 in the New Testament. Interestingly, the Book of Isaiah has 66 chapters, the first 39 of which focus on the Law and the last 27 emphasizing grace. Throughout Isaiah we find the reference to *the Holy One of Israel* 25 times.

Some have argued that at least three different men wrote the Book of Isaiah. This is somewhat troublesome in that it leads to the impression that God's Word is put together in a way that's somewhat deceptive. However, when the Dead Sea scrolls were discovered, the scroll of Isaiah had no breaks. It appeared as one long text written by one man. Isn't God faithful to be straightforward and clear?

Isaiah reaffirmed God's promises to Israel but also warned of punishment if His laws were not followed. His theme would be Isaiah 30:15—*This is what the Sovereign LORD, the Holy One of Israel, says: "In repentance and rest is your salvation, in quietness and trust is your strength."* Always Isaiah was calling the people to repent and turn from their wicked ways. God's promises were of salvation, and His warnings were of judgment. Isaiah foretold that the Messiah would rein over a remnant of the people and that then Judah and Israel would be a holy nation. The tree of David had been cut down through sin, but the seed of Jesse would sprout a branch that would be the hope of the future.

So as we study the Book of Isaiah and begin to understand its contents, Isaiah himself will bring the message as he predicts, portrays, and proclaims the Word of the Lord.

*Written by Linda Shaw*

# Isaiah

■ A Study of Isaiah, Chapters 1—4

**LESSON 1**

---

## DAY ONE

# Rebellion Repaid

**Read Isaiah 1, concentrating on verses 1-9. Read 3:1-15.**

1. Who were the four kings during the time of Isaiah's vision, and for whom was the vision intended?

2. Summarize the meaning of Isaiah 1:2-3.

   *Judah Israel*

3. How are the people described in verse 4, and what are the three indictments against them?

   *Sinful
   Turn backs on God
   Corrupt*

4. Fill in the blanks: *Your whole head is _____, your*

   *whole _____ _____ (verse 5).*

5. How do verses 7-9 describe the land and cities?

   *devoured
   Desolate*

6. Isaiah warns the people that unless God had left them a few survivors, they would be like Sodom and Gomorrah. What were the sins of Sodom? See Ezekiel 16:49-50.

7. What does Isaiah say in 3:1-9 that God's judgment will be on Judah and Jerusalem?

8. Fill in the blanks: *Tell the _____ it will*

   *be _____ _____ _____, for they will enjoy*

   *the _____ of their _____ . Woe to the*

   *_____! _____ is upon them! They will be*

   *_____ _____ for what their _____ have*

   *done (3:10-11).*

9. *The Lord takes His place in court* and does what (3:13)?

---

Isaiah takes one verse to give us the background of who he is, who the kings are during his prophecy, and for whom the prophecy is intended. Then he gets right to it and presents the case of God against his rebellious child, Judah: *Hear, O mountains, the LORD's accusation; listen, you everlasting foundations of the earth. For the LORD has a case against his people; he is lodging a charge against Israel* (Micah 6:2). The northern kingdom of Israel is about to be overrun by Assyria and will no longer be independent due to her rebellion. Isaiah is pleading God's case that Judah could be next.

Even a dumb animal knows who its master is, but does Judah? I have a nine-year-old dog named Missy. She is a mutt disguised as a small black Labrador. It drives my children crazy that when I'm home she sticks by me. Wherever I go in the house, she follows. If I go to the backyard, she's on my heels. When I'm in the front yard, she lies in the doorway to watch me until I return. She's in the kitchen while I work. Why? Who feeds her and bathes her, takes her for walks, and drives her to the vet when she's ill? Missy may be a dumb animal, but she knows who her master is.

Isaiah is telling the people that they are not as smart as their own animals. They do not know their master. They do not know their God. *Even the stork in the sky knows her appointed seasons, and the dove, the swift and the thrush observe the time of their migration. But my people do not know the requirements of the LORD* (Jeremiah 8:7).

The people are sinful, corrupt, and rebellious. Beatings were the plight of lawbreakers, but Judah's sins were so great that there was no place left to strike her. Isaiah 1:6 refers to this when it says from head to foot nothing is sound. Wounds, welts, and open sores are found on every available spot; yet the rebellion continues. The beatings have not brought her to her senses.

If God were not gracious to leave a few survivors, the remnant, then Judah would end up like Sodom and Gomorrah. These cities were completely destroyed by fire for their evil. Ezekiel 20:35 warns, *I will bring you into the desert of the nations and there, face to face, I will execute judgment upon you.* He will take the people out of their country to face their judgment unless they leave their sin and return to God.

As we move to Isaiah 3, the theme remains the same. The Lord of Hosts will remove the leadership from Jerusalem and Judah. This is due to the corruption of those in charge. *Both hands are skilled in doing evil; the ruler demands gifts, the judge accepts bribes, the powerful dictate what they desire—they all conspire together. The best*

*of them is like a brier, the most upright worse than a thorn hedge. The day of your watchmen has come, the day God visits you. Now is the time of their confusion* (Micah 7:3-4). So poor will be the leadership that if one has a cloak, which will obviously be scarce, then he can be the leader. But he will refuse, for no one will want to lead such a mess (Isaiah 3:6-7).

10. The sorrow of it all is that the simple obedience of the people would bring God's promises. Record Deuteronomy 28:1 below, and then list the blessings God's people were promised through obedience in Deuteronomy 28:2-14.

Instead of blessing, today's scripture ends with the promise of judgment. Isaiah 3:13 declares, *The LORD takes his place in court; he rises to judge the people.* The leadership has failed the people, and they have followed this example. The poor have been oppressed, and no one cares. God will not tolerate this. The people will be repaid for their rebellion.

The theme of Isaiah and much of the Old Testament is simplified in today's study. God has set out His laws. They are to be obeyed and will bring the people fulfillment of all God's wonderful promises. But rebellion will not be acceptable—it will be repaid. Sin will be punished. Yet God will not totally wipe out His nation, His people. There will always be a remnant to carry on. May we be part of the remnant who choose to obey and to take time to know our Master, who gives us every good blessing from His hand.

## DAY TWO

# Religious Rituals

**Read Isaiah 1:10-15.**

1. How would you summarize the contents of today's scripture?

   *Going through the motions*

2. The religious rituals of the people were not pleasing to God. From the following scriptures give a possible reason.

   1 Samuel 15:22

   Amos 5:21-24

3. What does God require of His people?

   Jeremiah 7:21-23

   Hosea 6:6

4. What is pleasing to God?

   Psalm 24:4-5

   Isaiah 66:2

   Hebrews 11:6

5. In Jesus' day lived a group whose behavior Jesus greatly opposed. Matthew 23:1-32 tells the story. Tell who they were and give reasons why He was so angry with them.

6. What can we learn from Jesus' story of the Pharisee and the publican, found in Luke 18:9-14?

7. What do you think Jesus might say to you if He came to speak at your church next Sunday morning?

"Ritualism when not backed up by righteousness is revolting to the Holy One," wrote Ralph Earle in *Meet the Major Prophets.* Going through the motions is not good enough, for righteousness is not about outward appearance but about the condition of the heart. Can we fool God? We may look good to each other when we're really hiding deceit and evil, but God is not fooled. He can see straight into the heart and know its true condition: *Do not be deceived: God cannot be mocked. A man reaps what he sows* (Galatians 6:7).

For whom do we live our lives? Is it for our friends, neighbors, and relatives? As long as it looks righteous to them, are we all right? What would today's scripture teach about this? Or do we live our lives for God and therefore try to please Him? Do we try to live in the Spirit and move as He commands? Do we confess as He convicts and turn and be changed as He instructs?

Jesus was always loving and accepting of any person who came to Him in sincerity. Whether it was a demon-possessed person, the rich young ruler, a tax collector, or the woman caught in adultery, Jesus always addressed the person's need and gave him or her opportunity to let Him fill that need.

But the group He was not tolerant with was the Pharisees, who had the religious rituals down pat, but not godliness. They did not care about people entering the kingdom of heaven. Rather, they cared about laws, power, status, and wealth—the very things Isaiah had condemned and warned about centuries before them. These men were not seekers of righteousness but seekers of good appearance.

Does this still exist in the Church today? Do we worry more about appearing righteous than about being righteous? Do we have a form of godliness but deny the power thereof? Are our hearts pure and holy, sincere in seeking Him?

J. Vernon McGee in his commentary on Isaiah[1] insists that the fall of a nation follows three steps. First is spiritual or religious apostasy. This is what Isaiah is warning Judah about. It is religious rituals with no true holiness. Then the nation falls into moral depravity. Again Isaiah began to talk with the people regarding their sins and idolatry. Finally, political anarchy comes. It happened several times to Israel and then Rome. Could our nations be next?

Have you ever been hurt by someone who claims to be religious? What saves each of us from acting that way? Only the Holy Spirit, who lives within us and convicts us of our sin, gives us the power to grow more like Jesus. Then the rituals of religion become a part of the journey, not the focus—and we stay close to God, not far from Him. This is pleasing to God and is His desire for each of us.

If you feel the rituals have become more important than righteousness itself, confess this to God right now. Then pray a prayer of recommitment to Him. Correct anything that He may lead you to do. Trust in His grace and forgiveness, which are necessary for holy living.

## MEMORY CHALLENGE

When should we extol (highly praise) the Lord?

## DAY THREE

# Repent

**Read Isaiah 1:16-17.**

1. In a dictionary or Bible concordance look up "repent" or "repentance," and write the definition.

2. "Repentance" has two components to its definition. Give one component from each of the following scriptures.

   Jeremiah 25:5    *Turn Away Lord*

   Mark 1:4

   *Change your ways*

3. Isaiah 1:16 starts, *wash and make yourselves clean.* Then seven ways to do this are given. List them.

4. What did Samuel tell the children of Israel they should do to be delivered from the Philistines? See 1 Samuel 7:3.

5. Record 2 Corinthians 5:17.

6. What are some signs of true repentance?

   Matthew 3:8

   Luke 19:8

   2 Corinthians 7:9-10

   *Godly Sorrow*

Repentance is more than saying, "I'm sorry." That's a start, of course—we definitely need to confess. But repentance has a second component: turning from the sin. *Guideposts Family Concordance* defines "repent" as "to turn away from sin and change one's behavior."

Often we take the easy way out by confession only. The sin remains. This is not true repentance; it's an insincere repentance. A good example of this is a spousal abuser, one who follows the pattern of losing his or her temper and physically harming the partner. Often this is followed by tears of sorrow and asking for forgiveness. But often the anger builds back up, the person loses control, and once again physical violence erupts. This pattern can go on for years. The abused spouse can often fall into the trap of believing the person is really sorry and feel that each time he or she should forgive. But the abuser is not practicing true repentance, because he or she has not turned from sin. Possibly the abuser needs some help in anger management or in getting to the source of the anger so it can be dealt with. These are things God often has us process through instead of delivering us instantly. But to truly repent, the abuser must seek and follow such help until the violence is behind him or her. That is sincere, genuine, complete repentance.

Recently at a party I found myself talking very negatively about a neighbor. It started out innocently enough as I was saying something kind about another neighbor but got into a story that involved all three of us that was not very flattering to this one neighbor. I felt it was gossipy and critical of her character. At the time I simply felt bad about it, but later the Holy Spirit convicted me that it was sin. I confessed it to the Lord, and He forgave me, but He told me I needed to confess to those who heard the story. I argued a little. After all, I had confessed and was forgiven. But the Lord said, "Accountability—you won't be so anxious to sin like this again." It's true. After calling five people and humbling myself by confessing my sin, I will stop myself next time before launching in! I needed the second component of repentance—turning from my way.

When Isaiah told the people to repent, he gave them seven ways to correct their behavior. These were to be the signs of their repentance. Without them, the repentance was insincere. As we repent, we must remember to change our ways. As we are responsible to others regarding their repentance, we must also look to see that their repentance is sincere in that their behavior is changed.

W. E. Vine wrote, "True repentance leads to willingness and obedience, to listen to the voice of God and do His will."[1]

## MEMORY CHALLENGE

What should always be in our mouths?

## DAY FOUR

# Reason Together

**Read Isaiah 1:18—2:8.**

1. Read Isaiah 1:18 in three translations, and record your favorite here.

2. Isaiah 1:19 gives us promise of the *best from the land* if we are _____ and _____.

3. From today's scriptures describe what will happen to Jerusalem, *the faithful city* that *has become a harlot* (verse 21).

4. How will Zion and the people within her be redeemed (1:27)?

5. In the last days, why should the people *go up to the mountain of the LORD*? See Isaiah 2:3.

6. What do you believe *let us reason together* (1:18) means? Give an idea and then summarize the following scriptures.

   Psalm 119:59

   Romans 12:2

   Philippians 4:9

   1 Peter 1:13

7. How important do you believe it is for a Christian to learn to think for himself or herself? Have you ever seen people in authority abuse their position by telling people what to think? Whatever the denomination, shouldn't we *test the spirits* (1 John 4:1)?

Wouldn't it be wonderful if any question we came to in life were answered specifically in the Bible? Unfortunately, that's not the case. How do we correct the bad habit of a child? Why was a fine Christian man killed in a car wreck at age 33? Is it necessary to be baptized at birth, after conversion, or not at all in order to go to heaven? Is it sinful to work in certain occupations? How do we know for sure whom we should marry? Hundreds of questions we come to as we journey along are not answered specifically in God's Word. So how do we handle them?

First, we need to know God. If we know who He is and how He operates in the world, we have narrowed it down. To truly comprehend Him, we must know His Word. The more we're aware of His Word, the more we discern Him. Would you pretend to know a neighbor you've never spoken to? God offers so much of himself through His inspired Word—that's the place to begin.

Next, we need to learn to follow His Holy Spirit's leadings in our lives. He will tell us a kindness to render to someone in need or convict us of a sin. He will give us insight into another person, helping us love and accept him or her more. He will direct us to spiritual brothers and sisters and warn us of someone with evil in his or her heart. The Holy Spirit always points to the Father and is therefore a great Instructor regarding God. He will teach us about how to live a godly life.

These two foundations are a good beginning to know how to answer the tough questions of our lives. Could we say that God gives us enough to lead to Him but that we're left to do our own thinking and decision making? *Let us reason together* perhaps means "Let us think." We're the only creatures to whom God gave such an advanced brain. Certainly the purpose was usage. Therefore, it's obvious that God wants us to learn to think for ourselves based on His Word and the leadings of His Holy Spirit.

Most of us have been educated through repetition and memorization. But as we become mature adults, many questions will require thinking. We must practice it. We must grapple with tough questions, thinking through the question "What would Jesus do in this situation?" Can I find guidance in the Bible? Is the Holy Spirit directing me? Throw in some common sense, which is a treasure from God. Check it out with a trusted and godly friend. But learn to think—for we will not be strong if we rely on someone else to tell us what to think, believe, or do.

*When I was a child, I talked like a child, I thought like a child, I reasoned like a child. When I became a man, I put childish ways behind me* (1 Corinthians 13:11).

## MEMORY CHALLENGE

Read the memory challenge verse aloud three times, and then write some phrases of praise to the Lord.

## DAY FIVE

# Reckoning for the Arrogant

**Read Isaiah 2:9-22 and 3:16-26.**

1. Who will the Lord God have a day of reckoning against? See Isaiah 2:12.

2. Who alone will be exalted in that day?

3. The theme of arrogance is repeated in Isaiah 3:16-26. Who specifically does Isaiah prophesy against?

4. Contrast these women with the woman in Proverbs 31:10-31.

5. What does God's Word say about arrogance in general? Summarize the following scriptures.

   1 Samuel 2:3

   Psalm 101:5

   Proverbs 8:13

   Proverbs 18:12

6. Personalize four of the Beatitudes from Matthew 5 in the following form.

Blessed am I when I am _____,

for mine is _____ (5:3).

Blessed am I when I am _____,

for I shall _____ (5:5).

Blessed am I when I am _____,

for I shall _____ (5:7).

Blessed am I when I am _____,

for I shall _____ (5:8).

Arrogance is a belief in one's own importance. It is a feeling of superiority to others due to one's perceived great importance. In the eyes of the arrogant person, no one is as important as he or she is—not even God. That's why humility, gentleness, mercy, and purity, as mentioned in the Beatitudes, are in such contrast to the arrogant person.

Chuck Colson had been the White House "hatchet man" during the Richard Nixon administration of the early 1970s in the United States. "Tough, wily, nasty, and tenaciously loyal to Richard Nixon" had been *Time* magazine's description of the man who would supposedly run over his own grandmother to reelect the president. Colson believed in the "almost sanctified notion that man can do anything if he puts his will in it."[1] His life revolved around pride in his own accomplishments.

Colson states, "The more I thought about it, the more one word seemed to sum up what was important to me. Pride."[2] Selected years before to deliver the valedictory speech for his high school graduating class, he noted that "pride was the keynote of my speech."[3] Pride was the reason he joined the Marines. And pride was at the heart of his service to the president and his willingness to use any means or method to accomplish his goal. Chuck Colson developed an arrogance that anything goes if it's for "the good of the country."

But Colson had a twinge of conscience along the way that some of the things he did to accomplish his goals were unethical, even illegal. Yet he rationalized that they were acceptable since, in his opinion, the ends justified the means. "I reflected back on the men with whom I served—Haldeman, Ehrlichmen, Mitchell, Nixon. They had been trapped as well—by their own pretensions of power."[4]

Yes, Colson was arrogant. He thought he was also safe, for he was sure the president could protect him. But the day of reckoning came. Watergate broke in the press, and then the Senate hearings took place. Eventually the reckoning went to the top, and Nixon was virtually forced to resign. He avoided prison only by the pardon of Gerald Ford, who took over as president. But others, including Colson, did go to prison.

No longer arrogant, Colson was a broken man. Everything he had believed in, fought for, ran over others for was gone in a day, in a moment. He had been wrong. He had been heady with power, pride, and arrogance.

Colson's story has a happy ending. Not only did his arrogance and aggression make headlines but also his conversion. His decision for Jesus Christ hit Washington with unbelief. With his reputation, who could believe he was sincere? But Colson's years of ministry in prisons since his conversion has confirmed his sincerity and honesty. Very likely none of this would have come about without Colson's time of reckoning for his arrogance.

The women in today's scripture had become worldly. Some of their dress imitated the priestly vestment and some idolatry. The dress specifically described was like the heathen goddess Ishtar. This is in contrast to the woman of virtue found in Proverbs 31. She was an industrious servant for her family as well as pure in character. Our dress and how well we care for ourselves reflect our hearts. Wanton dress indicates one of spiritually bankrupt character. Dress of good taste, whether stylish or not, reflects wholesomeness. Which do you think would be pleasing to God?

God never tolerates the arrogant. How could He? They have put themselves in His place. Instead, He brings them low to know their proper place in His order of things. As with all sin, arrogance will be punished. The discipline may come quickly and with great embarrassment. Let us not be caught in arrogance, but humbly serve our God.

## MEMORY CHALLENGE

Fill in the blanks:

*I will _____ the _____ at all _____;*

*his _____ will _____ be on my*

*_____.*

Psalm 34:1

# Remnant

**Read Isaiah 4.**

1. *In that day the Branch of the LORD will be*

   _____ *and* _____ (4:2).

2. What will the fruit of the land be?

3. What will those left in Jerusalem be called?

4. What is the definition of "remnant"? Look it up in a dictionary or Bible concordance, along with Isaiah 1:9.

5. God has always promised to leave a remnant of His people. Summarize the following verses regarding the remnant.

   Isaiah 10:20

   Isaiah 37:31

   Jeremiah 23:3

   Micah 7:18

   Zephaniah 3:13

   Romans 9:27

Isaiah 4 deals with God preparing a few survivors of His people to be the righteous, chosen remnant. This is called "remnant theology."

Mainline Jews also combated the drift toward paganism by stressing remnant theology. In other words, they declared that God would preserve a faithful remnant of His people who would be the seed of a new Israel. For the first time, they entertained the notion that not all Jews were the chosen of God. To be a true Israelite, a person had to obey the law of Moses.

From the very beginning, God had revealed that His people must obey Him. History proved that any of Abraham's descendants who rebelled against God failed to receive His blessing (for example, Esau and Ishmael). So God had always required obedience. But the Exile drove the point home.[1]

Sending prophets also drove the point home. Isaiah, Jeremiah, and Ezekiel can lay claim to one-third of the references in the Bible to the remnant. Isaiah spoke several times of the remnant, presenting it as both a warning and a promise. The people would lose their blessing, including safety, their land, their worship, productive crops, and numerous children, if they disobeyed. The situation could become so bad, Isaiah warned, that the country would be overrun, and God would leave only a few behind to be the remnant. But the remnant promised that Israel would always have a representative. God's chosen children would never be totally wiped out. There would be a small seed of people from which God could resurrect a great nation. So the remnant represented great hope.

Isaiah 4:4 speaks of the remnant being holy in that their filth would be washed away, which is the outward cleansing. This is the spirit of judgment, which brings justification. Then there would be the purging of stains, which is inward purity. This is the spirit of burning, which represents sanctification.

With the evil and threatening times in which Isaiah was prophesying, the people needed the promise of a remnant. The nation was disobedient and threatened to be overrun by the giant enemy Assyria. Was there any hope? If the nation repented, God would continue to protect and bless. But if the nation did not turn from their evil ways, God would leave a small handful of the faithful, holy people, who would represent Him and in time would again grow to a nation of His people.

The Book of Revelation speaks of the remnant: *those who obey God's commandments and hold to the testimony of Jesus* (12:17). In other words, if we choose to be followers of God's laws and the teachings of His Son, Jesus Christ, we're part of the present-day remnant. We're part of those who choose obedience and blessing. We may be few, but we hold great promise. What a blessing!

*Written by Linda Shaw*

Write out Psalm 34:1 from memory.

# Isaiah

■ A Study of Isaiah, Chapters 5—6

## DAY ONE

# Song of the Vineyard

**Read Isaiah 5:1-7.**

1. What did the owner do to prepare the vineyard as described in Isaiah 5:1-2?

2. What questions did Isaiah, the singer, ask about the vineyard (verse 4)?

3. What is going to happen to the vineyard?

4. Summarize a similar story Jesus told in the parable of the landowner in Matthew 21:33-44.

5. What is the interpretation of the song of the vineyard given us in Isaiah 5:7?

6. What similarities do you see in Psalm 80:8-19 with the song of the vineyard?

Everyone in Jerusalem was at the vintage festival celebrating. The grapes were harvested, and now it was time for rejoicing. One by one, musicians would sing their songs, and those who knew them would join in. The crowd was laughing and applauding and generally enjoying themselves. In this atmosphere Isaiah's turn came, and everyone was attentive. Unknown to them, Isaiah had a message the Lord had put on his heart that carried rebuke, but what a good hearing it received! Nothing more important happened that day.

The vineyard is in a great location, with fertile soil rich in minerals. The ground is well turned and the stones have been removed. The vineyard is generally well tended. The highest-quality vines have been planted that should have produced luscious, dark, purple grapes. A hedge and wall were built around the vineyard, with a watchtower to guard it from thieves. The wine-vat is ready for the grape pressing. The owner has neglected nothing; he has invested well. He has done everything for a good return on his investment. But when the harvest comes, the owner finds *worthless [grapes]* (Isaiah 5:2, 4, NASB) that are puny and bitter.

## MEMORY CHALLENGE

# Psalm 34:2

*My soul will boast in the LORD;
let the afflicted hear and rejoice.*

Could the owner have done more for the vineyard? Simply no. At the end of the song, Isaiah declares that the vineyard is Israel and Judah, who are *the garden of his delight.* But instead of the justice and righteousness of good fruit, God has received only bloodshed and distress.

God had given Israel laws for boundaries, the Temple for worship, holidays for rejoicing, leaders to guide the people, prophets to exhort, history to remember, and choice land for earthly success. But "where pruning and cultivation fail, nothing of real value grows."

God is telling His people through Isaiah in the song of the vineyard that He will remove His protection, forsake it to its own sin, withdraw His blessings, and place it at the mercy of anything by taking away its hedge. Downfall did not come to the divided nation of Israel without warning. The people simply chose to ignore the message of God.

Isaiah got up in a crowd of people on a day of celebration and sang a song of gloom as a warning. That took some courage and obedience, two of the very elements the people he was singing to lacked. How did he do it?

7. How do you sing a difficult song during a time when there's supposed to be celebration?

8. Summarize from the following scriptures what you learn about singing.

   Psalm 59:16

   Acts 16:25

   Ephesians 5:19

9. Read the song of Moses and Israel in Exodus 15:1-18. Use the following space for any notes needed.

10. How do we learn to sing a song whether celebrating or in crisis? Another way to ask this question would be, "How do we learn to rejoice daily regardless of whether things are going well or badly?"

"Discipline brings delight," writes Jeannie McCullough, teacher and founder of Wisdom of the Word Bible study. Singing a song may come naturally when life is blessed, but in prison, in sickness, or before crossing the Red Sea with the enemy at one's back is not an easy time to sing. To be prepared to sing in the hard times, a person must discipline himself or herself to sing.

Jeannie states there is the discipline of abstinence. This includes solitude and silence, which are meditation, fasting, frugality, chastity, and sacrifice. Then she refers to the discipline of engagement. Study, worship, celebration, service, prayer, fellowship, confession, and submission are on this list. As we give ourselves to God and incorporate discipline into our lives, we receive structure and substance. Discipline is the backbone of holy living, which then opens the floodgates for God's blessings. *Blessed are they who maintain justice, who constantly do what is right* (Psalm 106:3). As we discipline ourselves in the Lord, He brings delight into our lives.

Our culture encourages delight first. "You deserve a break today," one popular advertiser tells us. But God tells us delight is a result of our discipline in Him. How do we sing a song in front of the Red Sea, in prison, or in sickness? We discipline ourselves as the Holy Spirit instructs us. We become strong in Him with structure and substance to our lives. When hard times come, we still trust in Him. Even if we have to wait for the delight, we have the discipline to do so. The delight will come. It's no guarantee that life will be all melodies. Rather, it's a guarantee that we can make a joyous song out of our lives. We can sing a song no matter what the circumstances.

# DAY TWO

# Such Woe!

**Read Isaiah 5:8-30.**

1. Today's passage contains six woes. List each below by its verse. Then summarize the corresponding verses. *(The Living Bible may be helpful in finding your answers.)*

   *a.* **Isaiah 5:8**

      Luke 12:15

   *b.* **Isaiah 5:11**

      Proverbs 20:1

   *c.* **Isaiah 5:18**

      2 Timothy 3:13

   *d.* **Isaiah 5:20**

      Proverbs 2:12-15

   *e.* **Isaiah 5:21**

      James 4:13-16

   *f.* **Isaiah 5:23**

      Proverbs 15:27

2. In yesterday's lesson we reviewed the parable of the landowner. Turn to Matthew 23:13-36 and summarize what Jesus spoke shortly after this parable.

3. This passage of woes in Isaiah has consequences intermingled with it. According to the verses listed below, state the consequences.

   Isaiah 5:13

   Isaiah 5:14-15

   Isaiah 5:24

   Isaiah 5:25

4. Summarize the warning given to the people in 2 Kings 22:13.

Whether studying Ezra, Revelation, or Isaiah, we are given plenty of warnings regarding the consequences of sin. God with His loving heart seems to reach out and cry, "Please —don't go that way! It will only end in woe!" Repeatedly this theme is seen in Scripture.

This series of woes today warns of doom and ends with final divine judgments. They are intermingled in the passage, requiring close examination to see which are the warnings and what are the consequences.

The first woe describes greed or covetousness. Greedy land-grabbers were taking the small farmer's land, which was strictly forbidden in God's Law. Men were to have their land by family inheritance. But these greedy landowners disregarded the Law and ended up with so much land that they could not even see a neighbor's house. Not only were they being immoral in land grabbing, but possibly they were getting the farms by unethical means.

The Lord had a solution for this. Ten acres of land, capable of yielding 4,000 gallons of grape juice, would now produce only eight gallons. Ten bushels of seed would produce only one bushel of grain. Soon the landowners would not be able to live off the land and would have to abandon their homes.

The second woe denounces drunkenness, which must have been a problem in Judah, for Isaiah refers to it numerous times. This passage refers to carousers who begin drinking in the morning and keep it up all day. They are the ruin of the nation, for they are nonproductive. They are condemned for being self-indulgent and never noticing God. Their end will be exile, where they will die of hunger and thirst. The whole city of Jerusalem will fall into Sheol so the proud will be humbled, but God exalted.

Woe number three is the defiance of God. These people drag their sins along behind them as an oxcart, much as Marley did his chains in Charles Dickens's *A Christmas Carol.* Their falsehoods, which started out like little cords, have become strong enough to be ropes pulling the oxcart. Yet they dare God to show He has power and can perform mighty acts. They are simply mocking God and the idea that He can bring judgment.

The fourth woe speaks of moral confusion. These people have changed the moral order and live by a different value system than God gave them. They call evil good and good evil, light dark and dark light, bitter sweet and sweet bitter. In our day we would say that they call their sins "mistakes." They have lost their moral compass.

The fifth woe is the pride of people running their own lives, with no dependence on God. They do it themselves. These are the "wise guys" who display conceit and self-sufficiency and do not need God. They need to read Proverbs. Their end is destruction.

The final woe speaks to the injustice of life in Judah. They mix wine with business and lose sight of right. They justify the wicked for a bribe and take away the rights of the godly. This is reminiscent of the parable on prayer that Jesus told in Luke 18:1-8. *In a certain town there was a judge who neither feared God nor cared about men* (verse 2). But a little widow was determined to get justice, so she kept bugging him. Finally, to get her off his back, the judge gave her justice. While the parable is teaching us to persist in prayer and not give up, it also states that God will *bring about justice for His chosen ones* (verse 7).

Isaiah 5:24-30 tells us God's plan for Judah if they do not turn from the woes they are inflicting on each other. God will whistle to a hostile nation, summoning it to Judah. The invader will be sure and swift and the victory so easy that not even a belt on the invading soldiers will be undone nor a shoelace broken. The judgments will be like a devouring fire, a tremendous earthquake, a devastating army, young lions attacking prey, a raging tide breaking over rocks, and darkness as in Egypt during the plagues. Sounds like a time to be out of the country on business!

These judgments came to pass with the invasion of Babylonia by Nebuchadnezzar in 589 B.C. God always keeps His Word.

Such woe! All could be avoided with repentance. Where are you today with God?

## MEMORY CHALLENGE

Today's passage deals some with arrogance, just as last week's did. Shall we boast in ourselves? In whom shall we boast?

## DAY THREE

# Seraphs and Smoke

**Read Isaiah 6, concentrating on verses 1-4.**

1. *Beacon Bible Commentary* states that Isaiah 6 shows the four stages of creative worship. Give a one- or two-sentence synopsis of each stage.

   *a.* Contemplation or vision (6:1-4)

   *b.* Revelation or self-evaluation (6:5)

   *c.* Communion or divine-human encounter (6:6-7)

   *d.* Fruition of service or commission and commitment (6:8-13)

2. Looking more closely at today's verses, describe the seraphs, and repeat what they said.

3. Summarize the following scriptures regarding God's holiness.

   Exodus 15:11

   1 Samuel 2:2

   1 Chronicles 16:29

4. What is the glory of God? Use a dictionary or Bible concordance to define it. Then summarize the following scriptures, which are just a few samples of how His glory is manifest.

   Exodus 40:34-35

   Psalm 19:1

Psalm 108:5

John 2:11

5. What do you think the smoke in today's passage represents? Some hints may come from Exodus 20:18 and Revelation 15:8.

6. Questions 3, 4, and 5 give us a formula. Fill in the blanks: When we praise God for His _____, then we see His _____, and He blesses us with His _____. Our awareness of the power of God increases.

The background to Isaiah's vision is King Uzziah's godly reign of 52 years. He conquered the Philistines and the Arabians. The Ammonites had submitted with gifts. King Uzziah had strengthened Jerusalem. But his fatal error of pride is recorded in 2 Chronicles 26:16-23. He went into the Temple to burn incense on the altar, which was forbidden to anyone but the priest. Azariah, the priest, led 80 other priests in confronting the king, but it only angered him. So the Lord intervened and struck him with leprosy. He lived separately the rest of his days while his son Jotham reigned.

Isaiah is uncertain as to what will happen to Judah now that King Uzziah has died. He goes into the Temple, probably on the Day of Atonement, and looks up where Yahweh's throne is. Instead, he sees a visible replacement as the Lord himself is sitting on the throne. Isaiah was seized with the terror of what he saw. An unholy man among unholy people, he is somehow beholding the Lord God Almighty face-to-face. No person could do this and live. A hot coal purges his sin. Now purified, Isaiah can stand in the divine presence justified and without fear. Then he hears God say, *Whom shall I send? And who will go for us?* Without hesitation, in radical obedience, he answers, *Here am I. Send me!*

Isaiah could have been given a vision of the nation's shame, for they still sacrificed and burned incense on the high places. But instead, he was given a vision of the glory of God displayed by the smoke and a warning of the departing glory from the Temple. Nationally that glory never returned, but the vision of God remained.

## MEMORY CHALLENGE

Who shall hear and rejoice as we boast in the Lord?

# Sinner

**Read Isaiah 6:5-7.**

1. What was Isaiah's confession?

2. Did any other person ever have this reaction? Summarize the following scriptures.

   Job 42:5-6

   Daniel 10:8

   Romans 7:24

3. One of the basic tenets of the Bible is that we are all born with original sin. But just as the seraphs touched Isaiah's lips in this passage, God can touch our sin and make us clean. Record the following verses.

   Romans 3:23

   Romans 6:23

4. Record 1 John 1:8 by personalizing it. Then write the promise found for each of us in the next verse (verse 9).

5. Did God ever give humanity a promise about unclean lips? Write what you learn from Jeremiah 1:9.

6. Why did Isaiah feel he could not see the Lord and live? Summarize Exodus 33:18-23.

A vision of God brings us to the awareness of our own sinfulness when we're not living a life of holiness. When we see His purity, holiness, and glory, our shortcomings, weaknesses, and iniquities become so clear. If we see a vision of God, our cry would be about our own uncleanness.

Isaiah saw God and was pierced to the heart with his sin and the sin of his people, Judah. He identified with the evil of the nation of God and included himself in it. Could he have picked the phrase "unclean" due to King Uzziah's leprosy? A leper was called unclean and had to call this out—"Unclean! Unclean!"—if he or she were anywhere near people. Now Isaiah sees the uncertainty of his nation after Uzziah's death and goes into the Temple on the Day of Atonement with an open and seeking heart. What comes to him is a vision showing him the leprosy of his own heart and people. He chooses to call it unclean.

But the burning coal touched the prophet at the point of his greatest need. Isn't that where God always reaches down to us? "For such a contrite heart there was immediate mercy."[1] The pronouncement of forgiven sin released Isaiah from his burden. He had seen God, but there was a purpose in it, a call, and Isaiah would live to use his lips in the Lord's service.

If we are seeking God and He gives us a vision, we will see our own inadequacy for the task, our own sinfulness if we're not entirely consecrated to Him. Along the journey, if there's no sense of one's own sinfulness, there's no vision of the Father. As fallen creatures, we should be aware on a regular basis of any sin we may be harboring. None of us ever arrives at perfection on this earth, so not feeling conviction means we're not coming to God with an open heart to examine us. This will lead us into an unclean life. We must be aware of our sinfulness to receive God's grace and mercy. That seals our love relationship with Him, who extends to us such overwhelming compassion when we're still in sin.

Where are you today with God? Are there sins He puts His finger on in your life on a regular basis? Are you coming to Him with a humble heart asking to be shown where you fall short of His grace? He is faithful to reveal our sin to us, then extend grace and mercy so we may genuinely live. Jesus said, *I came that they may have life, and have it abundantly* (John 10:10, NASB).

Take a few quiet moments now to let God examine your heart so anything that's not right can be made right and so you may have the joy of the abundant life.

## MEMORY CHALLENGE

Jeremiah 9:23-24 is similar to Psalm 34:2. Summarize here.

## DAY FIVE

# Send Me

**Read Isaiah 6:8-9.**

1. Can you think of a time you felt the Lord ask for a servant and you said, "Send me"?

2. Summarize the following scriptures of other saints who asked to be the one sent.

   1 Samuel 3:1-10

   Nehemiah 2:1-5

3. Other saints struggled over being sent by God. Summarize the stories told by the following scriptures.

   Exodus 3:10-11; 4:1-5, 10-12

   Jeremiah 1:5-6

   Jonah 1:1-3

   Acts 9:10-17

4. Record in Ezekiel 3:10 what God said to another prophet.

5. When Isaiah said, *Send me*, what was God's message to him?

Hopefully when we have a vision of God, we're changed. True vision is transforming. Isaiah was a remarkable man in that the vision changed him immediately. He reacted at once with *Send me.* This is not always the case, even among saints as we studied today. Sometimes saying yes can be a struggle.

Maybe the struggles were many, including inadequacy, unwillingness, fear, lack of resources, or timing. But to come to the place that one says yes is to say, "Send me." "The true servant of God goes, because his heart prompts him in holy love to the task."[1] Eventually the saint is prompted to go by his or her love for God.

A vision of God is a stark contrast to the truth about ourselves. G. B. Williamson in *Beacon Bible Commentary* calls Isaiah's vision a "saving vision."[2] He says Isaiah saw God and then saw his own sinfulness. But immediately Isaiah experienced the grace of God so he could see the work assigned to him.

Each of us has a task God wants to "send us" on. It's probably not as difficult or all-encompassing as Isaiah's, but it's God's task for us. While Isaiah's task was to last a 50-year lifetime, ours may be more temporary. We may struggle to say yes. But God has a task for each of us, and a heart of love and commitment cries out, "Send me."

## MEMORY CHALLENGE

Fill in the blanks:

*My soul will _____ in the LORD; let the*

*_____ hear and _____.*

Psalm 34:2

## DAY SIX

# The Stump Remains

**Read Isaiah 6:9-13.**

1. Isaiah 6:9-10 is a hard passage to understand. What do you think it may mean? Matthew 13:10-17 may help you with your answer.

2. Summarize the following scriptures, which further relate to the above question.

   Deuteronomy 29:4

   Isaiah 42:20

3. When Isaiah is told the people will be insensitive, he asks, *For how long, O Lord?* (verse 11). What is the answer?

4. What is the stump?

5. Relating to the people who do not see or hear, how would the holy seed or stump be different from that and therefore be chosen?

6. "The stump" is a word picture of the remnant. Summarize the following verses regarding the remnant.

   Jeremiah 23:3

   Zephaniah 3:12-13

Romans 9:27

Isaiah 6:9-13 speaks of a spiritual choice we make to be tender toward the Holy Spirit. God has much to say to us, but we must be willing to listen and receive. For many reasons we often are not. The truth or message may be painful, too hard to carry out, not what we want to do, too sacrificial, or too frightful. But often we choose not even to get to the above situations by refusing to hear in the first place. Then those difficulties standing in our way don't have to be addressed at all. If we're not careful, a lifetime of being spiritually hard of hearing is the result.

Staying tender is a tough but rewarding job. Two sisters each had a daughter they loved very much. As is often the case, when the girls became adolescents and young women, they had issues to work out with their mothers. No parent is perfect even if he or she is a great parent; every relationship has problems that need to be worked out. One mother was controlling and felt the authority of the parent should not be questioned even when the child has reached adulthood. While her daughter tried to work out issues with her, she was unable to hear what the daughter said. "She doesn't listen" were the words of the frustrated and hurt daughter. Their relationship was a painful one. The daughter chose to avoid her mother in order to avoid pain.

The other mother made equally as many mistakes in the relationship with her daughter, but she was willing to listen. She had an openness about the fact that she was not perfect and had more to learn about parenting and relating to the people she loved. Although it was painful and sometimes felt unfair, she listened to her daughter. They worked out many issues between them. When the daughter was a young woman, they had become best friends. If a situation arose requiring the mother to assert her authority, the mother did it, but basically they were fellow close confidants on the journey of life. Their relationship was extremely rewarding and meaningful.

The second healthy and satisfying relationship was possible only because both mother and daughter were willing to listen. Theirs was an attitude of openness to learning new things in life to bring improvement and enrichment.

Is this not what God is saying to us in this passage?— "Hearing is not always easy, but it is necessary. Listen to Me. Listen, learn, and obey." God intends us to work out with Him our shortcomings that are less than pleasing to Him and that keep us from being truly Christlike. We cannot do this without listening.

Our hope is that no matter how far we get from Him, He will always leave a stump of promise and hope. He will not totally cut us or the tree down but will leave a part from which to build. There's always His promise of redemption and the hope of a holy life. There's always a stump. Maybe we have been hard-of-hearing in the past. Maybe we've carried it so far that only a stump remains, but He still calls to us to listen. *Come to me* (Matthew 11:28). "Return to Me. Be My holy seed."

Listening is a choice. Even if it has not been one of your choices in the past, you can start today. Listen to God and what He has to say to you. It's the only way to find a rewarding and meaningful life in Him. If this seems too difficult, begin praying where you are. Pray that He will make you willing to listen. He will take that stump of your life and make it into something incredibly beautiful.

*Written by Linda Shaw*

## MEMORY CHALLENGE

Write out Psalm 34:1-2 in the space below.

# Isaiah

■ A Study of Isaiah, Chapters 7:1—9:7

**LESSON 3**

*Lesson 3 is the study of Isaiah 7:1 to 9:7, a lesson on trusting God in all situations. May your belief and trust in God be strengthened as you apply this lesson to your daily walk with Him.*

## DAY ONE

# Trust God

**Read Isaiah 7, concentrating on verses 1-13.**

1. Name the kings and their kingdoms identified in today's passage. *Ahaz Rezin Aram & Pekah*

2. Summarize 2 Chronicles 28:1-4.

3. How did King Ahaz (the house of David) and his people react to the news that the Arameans were camped in Israel (Ephraim)?

4. What did the Lord tell Isaiah to say to Ahaz? Summarize Isaiah 7:4-7.

5. *Again the LORD spoke to Ahaz* (7:10). What did the Lord ask Ahaz to do? See verse 11.

6. How did Ahaz respond? See verse 12.

As the largest of the 12 northern tribes, Ephraim represented Israel (Hosea 5:3) and lay to the north of Judah. Aram (Syria) was north of Israel and Assyria north and east of Aram. The *house of David* (Isaiah 7:2) refers to the line of kings in Judah descended from King David—in this instance, King Ahaz.

The kings of Israel and Aram had formed an alliance against Assyria and wanted Judah, under an Aramean puppet king of their choosing, to join them. King Ahaz was a wicked king who did not serve the Lord (2 Kings 16:2-4; 2 Chronicles 28:1-4); he failed to trust God or believe His promise to King David that He would establish the throne of his kingdom forever (2 Samuel 7:12-13, 16). Therefore, Ahaz and his advisers reacted to the news of the plan with great fear and trembling. What a contrast to his ancestor King David, who wrote, *The LORD is my light and my salvation—so why should I be afraid? The LORD protects me from danger—so why should I tremble? . . . Though a mighty army surrounds me, my heart will know no fear. Even if they attack me, I remain confident* (Psalm 27:1, 3, NLT).

Another psalm expresses these thoughts:
> *You are my King and my God. You command victories for your people.*
> *Only by your power can we push back our enemies; only in your name can we trample our foes.*
> *I do not trust my bow; I do not count on my sword to save me.*
> *It is you who gives us victory over our enemies; it is you who humble those who hate us.*
> *O God, we give glory to you all day long and constantly praise your name* (Psalm 44:4-8, NLT).

Long-suffering and merciful, God was not yet ready to punish the people of Judah by allowing them to be taken captive. He sent Isaiah to meet with Ahaz and to reassure

## MEMORY CHALLENGE

# Psalm 34:3

*Glorify the LORD with me;*
*let us exalt his name together.*

him that he did not need to fear this alliance of his enemies. Isaiah was to take his son Shear-jashub to the end of
the *aqueduct of the Upper Pool, on the road to the Washerman's Field* (Isaiah 7:3). The Washerman's, or fuller's,
field was where the people of Jerusalem did their laundry
and laid it out to dry. The Gihon spring fed the Upper Pool,
and an aqueduct carried the water to a lower pool, which
supplied Jerusalem with water. Ahaz may have been attempting to supervise the diversion of the water supply
from outside the wall of the city through an aqueduct to
the inside of the city to secure it and prevent it from being
taken by the enemy. Later, King Hezekiah was successful
in completing the project (2 Chronicles 32:3-4, 30). The
name of Isaiah's son, Shear-jashub, means "a remnant shall
return," a reminder that God has always had a remnant
who have remained true to Him.

Despite the iniquity of King Ahaz, God assured him that the
two northern kings were merely two smoldering stubs of
firewood, little sticks with smoke but no fire, and their plans
would fail. He told Ahaz to be calm and not to fear. With the
promise came a warning: *If you will not believe, you surely
shall not last* (7:9, NASB). Distrust leads to distress!

Knowing that Ahaz was unfaithful (2 Chronicles 28:22),
unbelieving, and planning to seek help from the king of Assyria, the Lord invited Ahaz to ask for a sign, a miracle, to
confirm His promise and to strengthen Ahaz's faith.
There's great power in faith! "Faith is encouraged and
strengthened by difficulties. Faith faces what to the natu-
ral mind are impossibilities, and resting on the promises of
God, relies on Him to fulfill His counsel concerning them
and to turn the obstacles to account for His glory."[1]

But Ahaz had made up his mind to follow his own counsel
and put his trust in Assyria rather than in God (2 Chronicles 28:16; 2 Kings 16:7). His answer, *I will not ask; I will
not put the LORD to the test* (7:12), was a hypocritically pi-
ous reference to Deuteronomy 6:16—*Do not test the LORD
your God.* Ahaz did not want a miraculous confirmation
that Isaiah's words came from God. The result of Ahaz's
decision to reject God's counsel and enlist the aid of the
king of Assyria is recorded in 2 Chronicles 28:19-25.

With each decision we must make, God gives us this same
choice—to seek His will, to trust Him and His promises
found in His Word, or to ignore Him or refuse to follow His
will and guidance. When we find ourselves in a battle, attacked by the enemy, we can tremble with fear, depending
on our own resources, or we can place our trust in a loving Heavenly Father. Fully trusting in God brings peace
and assurance even in the midst of the storms of life, and
strength to face the battle. *Your faith [should] not rest on
the wisdom of men, but on the power of God* (1 Corinthians 2:5, NASB). Do you trust God in faith or tremble alone
in fear? Faith or fear? Trust or terror?

7.  Proverbs 30:5 assures us that *Every word of God is
    flawless; he is a shield to those who take refuge in*

*him.* Read Psalm 91. Record a phrase that has special
meaning for you, and share it with your group.

8.  Summarize the following verses on why we need not
    fear:

    Deuteronomy 31:6

    Psalm 46:1

    Isaiah 41:10

9.  Record the following verses, and underline the benefits
    of trusting God.

    Psalm 125:1-2

    Proverbs 3:5-6

    Isaiah 26:3

    Jeremiah 17:7-8

*O for a faith that will not shrink,*
  *Tho' pressed by ev'ry foe,*
*That will not tremble on the brink*
  *Of any earthly woe!*

. . . . . . . . . . . . . . . . . . . . . . . . . . . . . .

*A faith that shines more bright and clear*
  *When tempests rage without;*
*That when in danger knows no fear,*
  *In darkness feels no doubt.*

—William H. Bathhurst

# Trust God's Promises

**Read Isaiah 7:10-16.**

God told Ahaz to ask for a sign to assure Ahaz that he need not fear the northern alliance against Judah. Ahaz refused, saying with insincere piety, *I will not ask; I will not put the LORD to the test.* Ahaz preferred to depend upon the king of Assyria and his armies and gods rather than to trust Almighty God. Isaiah reproved Ahaz; he was not only trying the patience of Isaiah, but since Isaiah was God's prophet, Ahaz was trying the patience of God himself. *Therefore*, Isaiah told Ahaz, *the LORD himself will give you a sign* (verse 14).

1. According to Isaiah 7:14, what is the sign?

Isaiah's prophecies, as with many biblical prophecies, often have meaning for both the immediate future and the more distant future. The New Testament sheds light on these Old Testament passages, enabling us to see more clearly.

2. *a.* Read Matthew 1:18-25. Summarize the message of the angel to Joseph (verses 20-21).

   *b.* What is the meaning of the word "Immanuel"?

   *c.* Who is the fulfillment of this prophecy?

Throughout the centuries there has been some controversy concerning the word translated "virgin" ("young woman," RSV) in Isaiah 7:14. Some have argued that it refers merely to a young woman of marriageable age. David McKenna in *Mastering the Old Testament* tells that Martin Luther "offered one hundred guilders to anyone who could show any other place in Scripture where the same word is translated 'young woman' rather than 'virgin.'... We must be true to the text and consistent in our interpretation."[1] An early, pre-Christian Greek translation used the word that always meant "virgin." "Because Immanuel is one of the few names for which Matthew supplied a translation—*God with us*—it is clear that Matthew wished to stress that in the miraculous birth of Jesus there was a dimension of Isaiah's words appropriate only to Jesus."[2]

3. Read Luke 1:30-35 and write the angel's answer to Mary's question (verse 34) recorded in verse 35.

God promised Abraham a blessing that would come from his people to all peoples on the earth (Genesis 12:3). He promised David that his kingdom and his throne would be established forever (2 Samuel 7:16). God cannot lie—His promises are forever true (Titus 1:2; Hebrews 6:18). The purposes of God for His people will continue; a remnant will remain faithful to Him.

4. Summarize the following verses that affirm the fulfillment of these promises.

   Romans 1:2-4

   Romans 15:8

   Galatians 3:16

5. God promised Abraham that all peoples on earth would be blessed through him. According to these verses, who are the inheritors of this promise?

   Romans 2:28-29

   Galatians 3:7, 9, 14

   Ephesians 2:12-13

The New Testament has many wonderful promises for the believer. Jesus has promised to intercede for us with the Father (Hebrews 7:24-25). The believer has been promised light (John 8:12), wisdom (Luke 21:15), help (Hebrews 13:6), grace (Romans 5:20-21), peace (John 14:27; 16:33), joy (John 15:11), strength (Philippians 4:13), His constant presence (Matthew 28:20), and eternal life (John 3:16; 6:40).

6. What else is the believer promised according to John 14:16-17; Acts 1:8; 2:38; Romans 5:5; Galatians 3:14?

7. Have you experienced the fulfillment of these promises in your life as a follower of Christ? Be prepared to share a brief example with your group.

Fill in the blanks:

_____ *the* _____ *with me; let us*

_____ *his* _____ *together.*

                                        Psalm 34:3

# Trust or Tyranny

**Read Isaiah 7:17-25.**

When the Lord, through His prophet Isaiah, gave Ahaz the prophecy concerning the child who would be named Immanuel, it was more than just a prophecy of the Messiah. For the immediate future, a young woman who at that time was a virgin would marry and conceive and give birth to a son whom she would name Immanuel. Before his early childhood would end, the Assyrian armies would devastate the lands of Syria and Israel, and the alliance of the two northern kings against Judah would fall apart. The prophecy was fulfilled only a year or two after it was given. Hoshea conspired against King Pekah of Israel and killed him (2 Kings 15:30). The king of Assyria captured the people of Aram and killed King Rezin (2 Kings 16:7, 9), then captured and carried the people of Israel away into exile (2 Kings 17:6).

The Lord had told Ahaz, *If you will not believe, you surely shall not last* (Isaiah 7:9, NASB). But rather than believe and trust Almighty God, Ahaz preferred to trust the king of Assyria and his armies and gods.

1. *The LORD will whistle for _____ from the*

   *distant streams of _____ and for _____*

   *from the land of _____* (Isaiah 7:18).

2. What will be the diet of the people of Judah when the prophecy comes to pass (7:22)?

3. This had been a land of a thousand valuable vines. What would the land now produce (7:23-24)?

4. Read 2 Kings 16:7-9. What did Ahaz do that was a defiant insult toward Almighty God (verse 8)?

First-century Hebrew historian Flavius Josephus finishes the story as follows:

> King Ahaz . . . was so sottish and thoughtless of what was for his own good, that he would not leave off worshipping the Syrian gods when he was beaten by them . . . and when he was beaten again he began to honor the gods of the Assyrians; and he seemed more desirous to honor any other gods than his own paternal and true (G)od, whose anger was the cause of his defeat; nay, he proceeded to such a degree of despite and contempt [of God's worship], that he shut up the temple entirely, and forbade them to bring in

the appointed sacrifices and took away the gifts that had been given to it.[1]

Because Ahaz refused to trust God, he and his people would be punished. Judah would suffer under the tyranny of Assyria and would be required to pay tribute (2 Chronicles 28:20-21). The land that had been productive became desolate; the Egyptians ("flies") and the Assyrians ("bees") swarmed through the land, pillaging and destroying. Instead of flocks and herds, most families would have only one cow and two sheep. Food would be plentiful but would consist of the simple diet of the poor—soured milk and honey. Vines and crops would be replaced by briers and thorns; instead of cultivation and agriculture, they would have to hunt for food with bow and arrow. In regard to the imposed shaving referred to in verse 20, to shave a man was the ultimate insult and brought great shame; it indicated the removal of kingly authority and national independence. "Where a company of God's people departs from the right ways of the Lord, fruitless and noxious products are sure to develop, and there will be spiritual barrenness instead of fertility that glorifies God."[2]

Larry Richards writes, "In 1 Corinthians 10:11, the apostle Paul reminds us that the experiences of Israel were written for our instruction. We are to learn the truths about our own relationship with God by studying the relationship of God with Israel. What a vital truth we learn from the tragic consequences of Israel's failures to walk in God's image. How eager we should be to respond to Him so He could subdue our enemies and act on our behalf."[3]

5. Where have you placed your trust? Summarize Proverbs 3:5-6.

6. *Blessed is the man who trusts in the LORD. And whose trust is the LORD* (Jeremiah 17:7, NASB). Summarize the following verses:

   Psalm 22:4-5

   Psalm 118:8-9

   Isaiah 12:2

Is this your testimony? Have you claimed God's wonderful promise of salvation and eternal life? *God so loved the world that he gave his one and only Son, that whoever believes in him shall not perish but have eternal life* (John 3:16). Do you know Jesus as your Savior? *If we confess our sins, He is faithful and just and will forgive us our sins and purify us from all unrighteousness* (1 John 1:9). Praise the Lord!

**MEMORY CHALLENGE**

How does one *glorify the LORD* and *exalt his name*?

# Trust or Turmoil

**Read Isaiah 8:1-10.**

1. What were God's instructions to Isaiah in verse 1?

2. Who were the witnesses?

3. What name was given the son of the prophetess?

4. What will happen before the boy can *say "My father" or "My mother"* (8:4)?

Isaiah had predicted the collapse of the Aram-Israel alliance and submission of Judah to Assyria. Now he prophesies this event once more and again includes the birth of a baby, a son who would be born to Isaiah and his wife. The Lord instructed Isaiah to take a large scroll and write on it the name "Maher-Shalal-Hash-Baz." This was not a small roll of parchment, but a great tablet on which he was to write in large, common Hebrew characters that could easily be read. This suggests that the tablet was for public display so that its message would be recalled when the prophecy was fulfilled. It would be a legal document, a public record, witnessed by two people of standing in the community so people would know it was not written after the fact.

The people would have understood the significance of the child's name, which means "quick to the plunder, swift to the spoil." Damascus, capital of Aram, and Samaria, capital of the Northern Kingdom of Israel, would be crushed and ransacked as the result of the Assyrian assault. This would occur before the prophesied infant could say "Daddy" or "Mommy," approximately two years after his conception.

According to the *NIV Commentary*, "reliable witness" refers not necessarily to character but to position. Uriah was probably King Ahaz's high priest, who changed the temple worship at Ahaz's command to conform to the pagan practice in Damascus (2 Kings 16:10-16). We cannot be sure of the identity of Zechariah. Isaiah's prophecy was fulfilled as predicted in 732 B.C., when the king of Assyria and his armies defeated Damascus and Samaria (2 Kings 16—17).

5. Isaiah, who had been pronouncing judgment with a literal statement of fact, now begins to use a poetic picture. Name and describe the contrasting waters pictured in Isaiah 8:6-7.

6. What does "the River" represent?

Shiloah was a gentle stream of water that trickled into Jerusalem, providing its water supply. It flowed peacefully through a conduit from the Gihon Spring. Isaiah used it as a symbol of the grace and peace that Ahaz and his people had rejected when they refused to trust God. "The River" in the Old Testament refers to the Euphrates. This turbulent, flooding stream was a picture of the Assyrian army as it swept over the land leaving devastation and suffering. The people would be able to do nothing to resist the mighty force—no battle strategies, no human alliances, and no clever plans of defense. God's judgment on a disobedient people would be carried out. Aram and Israel would be totally inundated; Judah would be flooded, but only "to the neck," meaning that the capital city of Jerusalem would be spared by divine purpose, as it was the "head" of Judah, the land of the promised Immanuel. And a believing, obedient remnant would remain, and God would not forget His covenant people; He would be with them.

7. According to 1 Samuel 15:22, what is most pleasing to the Lord?

8. What does God require of us? Summarize these verses.

   Deuteronomy 5:32-33

   Deuteronomy 10:12

   James 1:21-22

9. Record the promise in Jeremiah 7:23.

We have this same choice—the gentle peace that comes from trusting and obeying God, or the raging turmoil that results from disbelief and disobedience, choosing self-will rather than God's will. All of God's promises include obedience on our part. David McKenna writes, "The promise of His comforting presence for the faithful has become the shattering punishment against the wicked. 'God with us' can be our hope or our fear."[1]

Radical obedience = "God with us," our hope, our comfort, and our peace in every situation. Praise His name!

Quote Psalm 34:3 aloud from memory.

# Trust and Obey

**Read Isaiah 8:11-22.**

1. What was God's warning to Isaiah in verses 11-12?

2. What will happen to Israel and Judah and the people of Jerusalem because of their failure to trust God (8:15)?

3. In verse 17 Isaiah says he will do two things. Name them.

What a devastating message the Lord had told Isaiah to deliver to the people of Judah! Apparently the king and his people not only rejected God's message but also turned against His messenger. Most prophets were viewed as traitors for not going along with the disobedient plans of Israel and Judah and because they predicted the defeat of the nations and their leaders. So God warned Isaiah not to give in to popular opinion and fear or dread of the northern alliance but to keep his trust in God and His Word.

As Christians in a secular, humanistic society, we see in God's Word His warning against allowing our culture to seduce or intimidate us. It has become popular in recent years to ridicule and denounce those who firmly believe that God means what He says in His Word. Even though a person is loving and caring, simply believing God's truths makes that person "politically incorrect." Remember how former United States vice president Dan Quayle attracted widespread public humiliation when he spoke out against the immoral message of a popular television program? But we must not allow fear to prevent us from speaking out against evil. Oliver Cromwell, who had the reputation of being very brave, once said, "I have learned that when you fear God, you have no man to fear."[1]

4. God tells Isaiah that He alone is to be feared and regarded as holy. What does Proverbs 1:7 tell us about the fear of the Lord? What do fools despise?

God is a sanctuary to those who obey His Word—a shelter, a refuge, and a temple: a place of holiness, peace, praise, and worship. To the disobedient, God becomes a trap and a snare, a rock that makes them stumble and fall.

5. Read 1 Peter 2:4-8. To whom does Peter refer to as *the living Stone?* What adjective describes what this Stone is to the believer? Why does the Stone cause the nonbeliever to stumble?

The people had rejected God's Law and spurned His Word (Isaiah 5:24), so God instructed Isaiah to write and seal His Law and His Word so that future events could authenticate them and future generations could study and learn from them. And we must pass on God's Word to our children and grandchildren, encourage them to read it and learn from it, and communicate to them our love of Scripture.

6. Isaiah affirms his willingness to wait on God to fulfill the prophecies according to His plans and timing. Do you wait on the Lord, or do you fail to trust Him and rush ahead of Him with your own schemes and solutions? Summarize the following verses.

   Psalm 27:14

   Psalm 130:5

   Habakkuk 2:3

Isaiah refers to himself ("Isaiah" means "Jehovah is salvation") and to his children with symbolic names of signs from God. In addition to his two sons, his "children" include all those who have remained faithful to God. Hebrews 2:13 applies this verse, Isaiah 8:16, to the spiritual children of God through Jesus Christ.

When we fail to trust God and wait on Him to work out our problems, we can end up in a mess as a result of our own poor decisions. This is what happened to the people of Judah. But instead of repenting and turning to God, they consulted spiritists and mediums, a practice God had forbidden (Leviticus 19:31; 20:6). Angry, distressed, and hungry, they saw only devastation and darkness. So they cursed not only their king but God as well. Do you blame God for the bad results of your own poor choices? Or do you repent and look for ways to grow spiritually through your failures?

*The Lord is my rock and my fortress and my deliverer; the God of my strength, in whom I will trust* (2 Samuel 22:2-3, NKJV). Amen!

On a separate sheet of paper, write Psalm 34:1-3 several times.

# Trust Jesus Christ

**Read Isaiah 9:1-7.**

Through the prophet Isaiah, God had pronounced judgment on His people. This was a time of deep distress and darkness. The Northern Kingdom had been devastated and its people taken captive by the Assyrian army. The land of Judah had been rendered desolate and unproductive, and the people were subject to the tyranny of the king of Assyria. But to the faithful remnant, God now gives a glorious promise. The stirring words of this passage are very familiar to those of us who have sung or listened to Handel's Messiah. Some of this promise has been fulfilled; portions of the promise will not be fulfilled until Jesus, King of Kings and Lord of Lords (Revelation 19:16) defeats the Antichrist and establishes His eternal kingdom of peace and righteousness.

Read each verse from this passage in Isaiah aloud, and then summarize or record the New Testament passages that correspond with the verse.

1. Read Isaiah 9:1; then summarize the following:

    Matthew 4:12-15.

Zebulun and Naphtali were two tribes of the Northern Kingdom located in the area of Galilee including the city of Nazareth. Jesus grew up in Nazareth, and much of His ministry took place in the area near the Sea of Galilee.

2. Read Isaiah 9:2; then summarize the following:

    Matthew 4:16

    John 8:12

    Ephesians 5:8

Not only was this a period of great darkness for God's chosen people, but from that time up to and including the time of Jesus' birth, the Jews were subject to the dictates and whims of foreign rulers. Into this darkness was born the Christ child, the Light of the World. Yet 2,000 years after His miraculous birth, it's still true that *the god of this age has blinded the minds of unbelievers, so that they cannot see the light of the gospel of the glory of Christ* (2 Corinthians 4:4).

3. Read Isaiah 9:3; then summarize the following:

    Luke 2:10

    John 15:11

    John 16:22

The believer rejoices in the presence and power and the majesty and glory of Christ as well *as the joy of [His] salvation* (Psalm 51:12).

4. Read Isaiah 9:4; then record the following:

    Matthew 11:28-30

When Gideon and his little band of 300 faithful men defeated the mighty Midianite army (Judges 6:33—7:25), God made certain that the victors knew that it was not by their might but by God's power that this was accomplished. Our Lord and Savior shatters our yoke of sin and helps us bear our burdens. We are able to accomplish all things not in our own strength but *through him who gives [us] strength* (Philippians 4:13).

5. Read Isaiah 9:5; then record the following:

    Revelation 21:4

The war implements and bloodied battle garments will be destroyed forever when Jesus returns to reign. His kingdom will be one of peace and prosperity (Psalm 46:9).

6. *a.* Read Isaiah 9:6-7; then summarize the following:

    Luke 2:11

    John 3:16

    Revelation 5:13

    Revelation 19:6

Immanuel of Isaiah 7:14 is the child of Isaiah 9:6, born in a manger in Bethlehem, the Son of God, Jesus our Lord. Fully human and fully God, He will reign forever in justice, righteousness, and peace.

   *b.* By what names will He be called?

The following observations are based primarily on commentary by Ross E. Price.[1]

Commentaries differ on whether "Wonderful" is a noun—one of Jesus' attributes, or an adjective describing Him as a Counselor who is wonderful. Price suggests it should be hyphenated, Wonderful-Counselor, referring to Jesus as "A Wonder of a Counsellor . . . a wonderful One who gave marvelous counsel and a marvelous One who gave counsel." He is the omniscient (all-wise and all-knowing) Counselor.

"Mighty God" derives from the Hebrew "El," which refers specifically to the Godhead. Only Jesus fulfills this attribute (Romans 1:4). He is the omnipotent (all-powerful) Deliverer.

"Everlasting Father" is actually "Father of Eternity." Jesus *was with God in the beginning. Through him all things were made* (John 1:2-3). His kingdom will be forever, and it is through Him that the believer receives the gift of eternal life (John 3:16). He is the omnipresent Comforter.

As Prince of Peace, Jesus will usher in the ideal and perfect kingdom. Not only will there be an absence of war and conflict, but all of His subjects will live together in rich and positive peace and harmony. He is the beneficent (good and loving) Ruler.

7. Read Isaiah 9:7. List three things about Jesus Christ that Paul records in Romans 1:1-4.

The human race has been *walking in darkness* and *living in the land of the shadow of death* (Isaiah 9:2) since Adam and Eve sinned by disobeying God (Genesis 3). We are able to praise God that we have *seen a great light. . . . a light has dawned* (Isaiah 9:2) if we know God's own Son, Jesus Christ, the Light of the World. If you have not confessed your sins and accepted God's merciful and loving gift of salvation through the shed blood of Jesus Christ, you're walking in spiritual darkness. Accept Jesus today as your Savior and Lord, and begin your walk in the light of His love.

Does this mean that a follower of Christ no longer experiences *walking in darkness* and *living in the land of the shadow of death*? Of course it doesn't. Even though no longer walking in spiritual darkness, even committed, obedient Christians will at some times in their lives experience emotional darkness. Perhaps your path right now seems to wind through dark shadows. There can be many reasons: the recent death of a loved one; the death of a marriage and a painful divorce; betrayal by someone you had loved and trusted; a wayward, lost child; depression; debilitating illness or chronic pain suffered by you or a loved one; loss of a job; an overwhelming disaster—and the list goes on.

Someday we'll live in a perfect world ruled by the source of light, the Prince of Peace. Satan, the prince of darkness, will have been defeated. But Paul reminds us that in our present world, our battle as Christians *is against the powers of this dark world and that you must put on the full armor of God, so that when the day of evil comes, you may be able to stand your ground* (Ephesians 6:12-13).

God doesn't cause the dark times in our lives—He is the Author of light. And he doesn't promise a quick fix. But He does promise Immanuel—God with us. When the way seems darkest and you feel most alone, Jesus is with you, walking beside you through those shadows. The shadows may cause His light to seem dim to you, but it's shining into the darkness, and it will guide you and comfort you as you trust in Him. *Weeping may go on all night, but joy comes with the morning* (Psalm 30:5, NLT).

> 'Tis so sweet to trust in Jesus,
>     Just to take Him at His Word,
> Just to rest upon His promise,
>     Just to know: "Thus saith the Lord."
>
> . . . . . . . . . . . . . . . . . . . . . . . .
>
> I'm so glad I learned to trust Thee,
>     Precious Jesus, Savior, Friend;
> And I know that Thou art with me,
>     Wilt be with me to the end.
>
> Jesus, Jesus, how I trust Him!
>     How I've proved Him o'er and o'er!
> Jesus, Jesus, precious Jesus!
>     O for grace to trust Him more!"
>                         —Louise M. R. Stead
>                 *Written by Helen Silvey*

## MEMORY CHALLENGE

Write out Psalm 34:1-3 from memory.

# Isaiah

**LESSON 4**

■ A Study of Isaiah, Chapters 9:8—12

*This lesson continues the prophecies given during the reign of King Ahaz, the prophecies that began with Isaiah 7:1. Some Bible scholars refer to this passage as "the Book of Immanuel." Through the prophet Isaiah, God continues to warn Israel and Judah of the punishments for their disobedience, inform Judah of the judgment on Assyria, and add more to the prophecy concerning the Immanuel of 7:14.*

## DAY ONE

# Reaping God's Anger

**Read Isaiah 9:8—10:4.**

1. To whom is this message addressed?

2. Had the people turned back to God in repentance for their sins? What was their attitude?

3. What will the Lord do to the elders (leaders) and the prophets who teach lies? Why?

4. According to verse 19, what will happen to the land and the people?

5. Will these punishments appease God's anger? Record the phrase on which you base your answer.

In this passage, Isaiah delivers the Lord's message for the Northern Kingdom of Israel. He is writing to Judah, using Israel as an example, warning of God's judgment on sinful nations. It is written in four stanzas of harsh judgments, each concluding with *Yet for all this, his anger is not turned away, his hand is still upraised.*

Assyria had conquered Israel, devastated the land, and taken most of the people into captivity. Yet those who remained continued in their *pride and arrogance of heart* (verse 9) and refused to turn to God and repent for their disobedience. In its arrogance, Israel believed it could recover and rebuild better than before, accomplishing this in its own strength. God had blessed the formerly united nations of Israel and Judah. He had intervened in their behalf in battles, protected them from enemies, and given them their land. Yet they failed to acknowledge Him. Have you been guilty of this same attitude and taken pride in your accomplishments, failing to acknowledge that it's God who has blessed you with your abilities? Pride and arrogance distance us from God and greatly displease Him. In James 4:6-7, we learn that *God opposes the proud but gives grace to the humble. Submit yourselves, then, to God.*

6. Record or summarize the following verses:

Psalm 101:5

Psalm 119:21

Proverbs 16:5

Proverbs 16:18

Proverbs 21:4

Isaiah 13:11

Malachi 4:1

Israel was attacked and devoured, crunched between enemies from the east and the west, *But the people have not returned to [God]* (Isaiah 9:13). Judgment continues; no one is spared, *for everyone is ungodly and wicked* (verse 17). Wickedness spreads like wildfire; its fuel is the people themselves. Civil war breaks out (the tribes of Manassah and Ephraim are both descendants of the sons of Joseph) and then turns against Judah. There is no justice—God's laws are ignored, and unjust and oppressive laws are made and enforced. The weak and defenseless are abused and defrauded. *Nothing will remain but to cringe among the captives or fall among the slain. Yet for all this, [God's] anger is not turned away, his hand is still upraised* (10:4). What a terrible judgment! What a terrible picture of life without God!

But the seeds of destruction lie in the sin itself. Just as Israel's wickedness burned and consumed her, we can be destroyed and our lives devastated as a result of the sin in our own lives if we refuse to turn to God in true repentance, and then live in radical obedience to His Word and His will. If there's sin in your life, turn to Him, who is *faithful and just and will forgive us our sins and purify us from all unrighteousness* (1 John 1:9), our Lord and Savior, Jesus Christ.

7. Read Psalm 51 and write out phrases to make up your own prayer.

*Search me, O God, and know my heart; test me and know my thoughts. Point out anything in me that offends you, and lead me along the path of everlasting life* (Psalm 139:23-24, NLT).

# Rendering Judgment

**Read Isaiah 10:5-19.**

1. God used Assyria to punish Israel, *to seize loot and snatch plunder, and to trample them down* (Isaiah 10:6), but now He accuses the king of Assyria of having a different purpose. What is it?

2. What city does the Assyrian propose to seize as he had Samaria and Damascus?

3. How many times did the king of Assyria say "I" or "my" in verses 8-11, 13-14?

4. What does the Lord say He will do after He has *finished all his work against Mount Zion and Jerusalem* (verses 12-13)? For what reason?

God had used Assyria as His instrument to punish His people in the Northern Kingdom. The Assyrians did not realize that their victory over Israel had been allowed by God as part of His plan to judge this *godless nation* (verse 6). The desire of the Assyrian king for world domination, including the conquest of Judah and Jerusalem, and his arrogant boasting eventually led to his own destruction—and it angered the Lord. The king boasted of the powerful cities that had fallen before his armies. God had not rescued Israel and its capital city of Samaria, so how could Jerusalem with its insignificant gods resist his powerful forces? But he did not understand God's purposes, and he underestimated God's power and might. God is omnipotent and sovereign, and He *was* and *is* and *will always* be in control!

5. What are the results of the foolishness of boasting against God according to the following verses?

   Isaiah 2:11

Jeremiah 50:31-32

Obadiah 2-4

Zephaniah 2:9-10

Luke 1:51-52

6. In Jeremiah 9:23, the Lord says not to boast of what three things?

7. Of what does Jeremiah 9:24 tell us we should boast if we do boast?

8. Look up "sovereign" in a dictionary or concordance, and write the definition.

Isaiah 10:12, 15-19 records God's response to the boasting of the Assyrian king. Isaiah reminds us that the tool or instrument is not greater than the one who uses it and that the "power of nations is no greater than the permission of God."[1] As Ross E. Price states, "The tail does not wag the dog."[2]

Geoffrey W. Grogan says that the forests and trees represent the Assyrian soldiers, who would be consumed by the Light of Israel, the Lord God Almighty. God does not light the fire; He is the Light that will become the fire.[3]

The army will be destroyed so utterly that even a child would be able to count the few soldiers that remain. The predicted punishment of Assyria took place a few years after their victory over Israel when the angel of the Lord destroyed 185,000 Assyrian soldiers (Isaiah 37:36). Later, As-

syria fell to Babylon and has never again been a powerful nation. The downfall of the capital city of Nineveh was also an act of God.

God will not tolerate arrogant pride in us because of our accomplishments or position and/or our failure to honor Him for His blessing and empowerment. In recent years we have witnessed the public humiliation of people who may have begun their ministries as God's humble servants but became impressed with themselves and committed the sins of pride, self-glorification, and self-promotion. It is a real and dangerous temptation for anyone whom God is successfully using in any kind of ministry, large or small. "Perspectives can be distorted by our accomplishments if we fail to recognize God working His purposes through us. When we think we are strong enough for anything, we are bound to fail because pride has blinded us to the reality that God is ultimately in control."[4]

*The foolishness of God is wiser than man's wisdom, and the weakness of God is stronger than man's strength* (1 Corinthians 1:25).

*Lord, forgive me for the times I have let myself and my pride get in the way of Your purposes. Sweet Holy Spirit, correct me when my perspectives become distorted by pride. In Jesus' name I pray. Amen.*

Do you need to ask God to forgive you for the sins of pride, self-glorification, and self-sufficiency?

## MEMORY CHALLENGE

Think of a time when God set you free from fear in answer to your prayer. Share with your small group if you're comfortable doing so.

# Righteous Remnant

**Read Isaiah 10:20-34.**

*The path of the righteous is like the light of dawn,*
*That shines brighter and lighter until the full day*
(Proverbs 4:18, NASB).

1. The remnant of Israel will no longer rely on whom?
   (For help with your answer, refer to 2 Kings 16:7, 9.)

2. On whom will they rely?

These were the people God had chosen as His children, people He had blessed and given the covenant promise that they would be a blessing to all the people on earth (Genesis 12:2-3). Yet they had turned away from God, refused to trust and obey Him, and instead put their trust in Assyria and its armies and gods. Sadly, this turning away from God has occurred in every generation. Today we live in an increasingly wicked and perverse world. For example, in the United States, originally founded on Christian principles and trust in God, many have turned away from God and deny His blessings, even ridiculing Christians for believing in God and His Word and relying on Him.

3. God's Word gives many warnings about the dangers of turning away from God. Record the warnings found in the following verses:

   Deuteronomy 4:9

   Jeremiah 17:13

   Ezekiel 33:12, 18

   Matthew 5:13

   John 15:6

   2 Peter 2:20-21

The prophet Isaiah assures the people of Israel that God's anger soon would be turned away from them and toward those who had struck them down. His judgment against Assyria would be total destruction. Isaiah's prediction would come true in his lifetime (Isaiah 36—37). A wicked empire might be used of God and have its day, but it would be destroyed and disappear, while the people of God would eventually prevail and continue to go down in history. However, the once-great nation, a people so numerous they were *like the sand of the sea* (Genesis 32:12), would be reduced to a mere handful of survivors who would return to God as a faithful remnant.

Isaiah pictures the advance of the Assyrian king and his army city by city as they victoriously march southward toward Jerusalem. But God has a word of comfort for the people of Jerusalem: they do not need to be afraid. The Assyrians may threaten and shake their fists in confidence and arrogance, but God will cut them down to mere stumps. The eventual destruction of Jerusalem would be from another source—Babylon—and in God's timing.

God has always had, and always will have, a righteous remnant who remain faithful to Him. Even during the time of the Great Tribulation, there will be believers who, though persecuted and martyred, will stay true to God (Revelation 7:13-14).

4. Psalm 15 gives us guidelines by which we may measure our lives according to God's standards for righteousness. *He who does these things will never be shaken* (Psalm 15:5). List these guidelines.

5. Jesus reduced these guidelines to two simple principles. Name them as recorded in Mark 12:30-31.

*Blessed are they whose ways are blameless, who walk according to the law of the LORD. Blessed are they who keep his statutes and seek him with all their heart* (Psalm 119:1-2).

6. How may we keep our ways blameless and be numbered among the righteous remnant? Match each Scripture reference with the phrase.

a. Psalm 112:1      ____ Don't let sin reign in your body.

b. Psalm 119:9      ____ Turn away from wickedness.

c. Psalm 119:11      ____ Obey God's commands.

d. Matthew 24:12-13      ____ Delight in God's commands.

e. Romans 6:11-12      ____ Stand firm; don't let your love grow cold.

f. Ephesians 4:11-15      ____ Believe that Jesus is God's Son.

g. Philippians 2:14-15      ____ Live according to God's Word.

h. Philippians 4:8      ____ Mature in Christ; hold steady.

i. 2 Timothy 2:19      ____ Don't complain or argue.

j. 1 John 2:6      ____ Hide God's Word in your heart.

k. 1 John 5:3      ____ Think praiseworthy thoughts.

l. 1 John 5:5      ____ Walk as Jesus did.

Colossians 1:9-11 is personalized below. Read it prayerfully.

*[I] have not stopped praying . . . and asking God to fill [me] with the knowledge of his will through all spiritual wisdom and understanding. And [I] pray this in order that [I] may live a life worthy of the Lord and may please him in every way: bearing fruit in every good work, growing in the knowledge of God, being strengthened with all power according to his glorious might so that [I] may have great endurance and patience.*

## MEMORY CHALLENGE

Fill in the blanks:

*I sought the _____, and he _____ me; he _____ me from _____ _____ _____.*

Psalm 34:4

## DAY FOUR

# Root of Jesse

**Read Isaiah 11:1-10.**

1. Who was Jesse? Read 1 Samuel 16:1, 10-13, to help you with your answer.

2. Who is the shoot, the Branch, about whom Isaiah is prophesying in today's scripture? (Refer to Jeremiah 23:5-6 and Revelation 5:5-9.)

3. *The Spirit of the LORD will rest on him—the Spirit of*

_____ *and of* _____,

*the Spirit of* _____ *and of* _____,

*the Spirit of* _____ *and of the*

_____ ___ _____ _____ (Isaiah 11:2).

4. How will He judge and render His decisions?

5. What is your understanding of the meaning of verses 6-9?

A once-beautiful bush in my yard appeared dead, the blooms gone and the few remaining leaves curled and brown. I cut the bare stalks down to the ground, promising myself that I would dig up and discard the roots when the temperature was more favorable. To my surprise and amazement, the next spring a green shoot sprang up from those supposedly dead roots, and within a fairly short time the bush was once again fruitful and beautiful. That restored bush is a good analogy of the prophecy of the Messiah recorded in today's passage. (Note: The word "shoot" comes from the Hebrew word *natzer,* which means "to shine or bloom." "Nazareth" and the term often used for Jesus, "the Nazarene" [Matthew 2:23], are also derived from this Hebrew word.)

Judah and the house of David would be cut down to a stump for their disobedience and rebellion toward God. But unlike Assyria, the root would only appear dead. God had promised David that his kingdom would endure forever (2 Samuel 7:16), and Isaiah prophesied that someday in the future there would be new life from the house of David in the person of the Messiah, Jesus Christ. This Branch from the Root of Jesse will judge with righteousness, justice, and faithfulness. His kingdom will be one of such peace and harmony that it will extend even to nature. The needy and defenseless, both human and animal, will no longer be at the mercy of the corrupt and powerful. The curse will be lifted! (See Genesis 3:14-19.)

6. Trace the line of Joseph, the earthly father of Jesus, in Matthew 1:1-17. In which verse did you find the names of both Jesse and King David? _____

   See Luke 3:23-37. Heli is thought probably to be the father-in-law of Joseph, which would make this the genealogy of Mary, the mother of Jesus. In which verses did you find the names of Jesse and David? _____

7. Who does Jesus say He is according to Revelation 22:16?

*The Spirit of the LORD will rest on him* (Isaiah 11:2). Matthew records this scene: *As soon as Jesus was baptized, he went up out of the water. At that moment heaven was opened, and he saw the Spirit of God descending like a dove and lighting on him. And a voice from heaven said, "This is my Son, whom I love; with him I am well pleased"* (3:16-17).

The sevenfold Spirit (Revelation 4:5; 5:6) can be compared to the lampstand of Exodus 25:31-32, 37. The center standard represents the Spirit of the Lord. The three pairs of side branches represent the three pairs of attributes of the Spirit: wisdom and understanding, counsel and power, and knowledge and fear of the Lord. These attributes define the character of Jesus Christ:

*Wisdom*—Jesus' wisdom is His ability to understand us intimately and totally and to guide us wisely and perfectly. Jesus *has become for us wisdom from God* (1 Corinthians 1:30).

*Understanding*—Jesus has not only knowledge of us in general but also spiritual discernment and sensitivity to our specific needs.

*Counsel*—Jesus is the *Wonderful Counselor* of Isaiah 9:6; He listens to our concerns and gives us wise and right advice. This also includes His ability to know and understand us.

*Power*—Jesus' power is that of the *Mighty God* of Isaiah 9:6. The Spirit of power includes mental and spiritual power as well as physical power. Jesus has the ability to bring things to pass and the ability to influence by example.

*Knowledge*—Jesus knows God the Father intimately and knows and understands God's Word (John 8:55). He also knows humanity (John 2:25) and our relationships with God and with others.

*Fear of the Lord*—Jesus' response to God—awe, trust, worship, and obedience—exemplified the fear of the Lord. He always obeyed God and His Word (John 6:38; 8:55; 14:31).

"In His humanity, [Jesus] went forth in the power of the Spirit. When He comes again (in His deity), He is going to rule in the power of the Spirit."[1]

## MEMORY CHALLENGE

On a separate sheet write Psalm 34:4 several times.

## DAY FIVE

# Reward for the Faithful Remnant

**Read Isaiah 11:10-16.**

1. What will the Root of Jesse be for the people and nations?

2. What will occur between Ephraim and Judah?

3. What will the Lord do to the gulf of the Egyptian Sea (Red Sea) and the Euphrates River?

4. What else will God provide for the remnant who return?

This portion of the prophecy about the Root of Jesse applies to both the near future for Judah and the distant future for all followers of Christ. The fulfillment of this prophecy began with the return of the exiles to Judah from Babylon and will be completed when Christ returns to reign over the earth.

5. Record Mark 13:26-27.

Jesus is a banner to attract all peoples and nations to himself. From the time of His earthly ministry, the Cross and the crucified and risen Christ have lovingly called people from every corner of the world to Him and through Him to the Father. At the end of this present age, Jesus will bring back to the Promised Land, from the four quarters of the earth, the remnant of God's chosen people. Israel became a nation in 1948, and its settlers have indeed come from every direction. This may be the beginning of the return of the remnant prophesied in this and other passages of Scripture.

The people of Judah were defeated not long after this prophecy by Isaiah and were taken captive to Babylon (2 Chronicles 36:15-20). Babylon was conquered a few years later by Persia. Seventy years after their capture by Babylon, King Cyrus of Persia issued a decree allowing the exiles to return to Jerusalem to rebuild the Temple. Many had become established, and some even prominent, and remained in Persia, but a small remnant returned to Judah and the city of Jerusalem. The complete story of other groups who eventually returned, the rebuilding of the Temple, the confession of sin and repentance of the people, and the restoration of Jerusalem can be read in the books of Ezra and Nehemiah.

God promised that He would make the way home easier and less hazardous for the returning remnant. Ephraim and Judah would be reunited, and their enemies would be defeated. God would dry up the Red Sea as He did when the Israelites fled from the Egyptians (Exodus 14:21-22). The mighty Euphrates would be reduced to seven shallow streams, and a highway would connect Assyria and Israel.

6. On the day when Jesus Christ returns to reign over the earth, the faithful, believing remnant will enter into God's glorious rest! And He again provides a highway, a highway "found only by following God."[1] Summarize Isaiah 35:8-10.

7. *Only the redeemed will walk there, and the ransomed of the LORD will return* (Isaiah 35:9-10). Look up "redeem" and "ransom," and record the definitions.

   Redeem—

   Ransom—

8. Who are the ransomed and redeemed? Record these verses. (If possible, use the NIV or NASB translation.)

   Romans 3:23-24

   Ephesians 1:7

   Colossians 1:13-14

1 Timothy 2:5-6

1 Peter 1:18-19

9. Is Jesus your Redeemer? Have you been ransomed from your sins through the blood of Jesus Christ? Can you declare with the confidence of Job, *I know that my Redeemer lives, and that in the end he will stand upon the earth* (Job 19:25)? Read Acts 3:13-20, and summarize Acts 3:18-20.

*May God himself, the God of peace, sanctify you through and through. May your whole spirit, soul and body be kept blameless at the coming of our Lord Jesus Christ. The one who calls you is faithful and he will do it* (1 Thessalonians 5:23-24) Amen!

## MEMORY CHALLENGE

Judah feared Ephraim and Syria and then feared the Assyrians. What do you fear? Make a list and include every fear, from the largest to the ones that may seem insignificant. Commit each one to the Lord, asking Him to deliver you from it and give you peace.

# Rejoicing Praise

**Read Isaiah 12.**

*Sing praises to God, sing praises; sing praises to our King, sing praises. For God is the King of all the earth; sing to him a psalm of praise* (Psalm 47:6-7).

What a fitting climax to the prophecy of a Messiah—the Immanuel, Wonderful Counselor, Everlasting Father, Prince of Peace of the preceding chapters! Isaiah 12 is a hymn composed of two portions of joyful and triumphant praise to the Lord. Each begins *In that day* and refers to the promised deliverance.

1. What does Isaiah say has happened to God's anger?

2. Isaiah praises the Lord as his _____, his _____, and his _____.

3. In verse 4 Isaiah records a number of things to do in that day. List them.

Isaiah is prophesying of the joy in the Lord the faithful will express in that day. But *I will praise you* does not refer to just a one-time event in the future. The blood-bought redeemed of the Lord should praise Him continually, now, and for eternity. Isaiah has total confidence and trust in the Lord and praises Him not simply for providing salvation, but because He *is* our salvation.

*With joy you will draw water from the wells of salvation* (Isaiah 12:3). Jesus Christ gave His life to be your salvation. Have you given your life to Him? He is the bottomless well of living water that never will run dry, and He extends this invitation: *If anyone is thirsty, let him come to me and drink. Whoever believes in me, as the Scripture has said, streams of living water flow from within him* (John 7:37-38). *Whoever drinks the water I give him will never thirst. Indeed, the water I give him will become in him a spring of water welling up to eternal life* (John 4:14). Accept His gracious offer of *living water* today, and experience the joy His salvation affords.

4. Scripture from Genesis to Revelation records songs of praise to the Lord. Many are found in Psalms. Read the following passages of praise from Psalms, and record a phrase from each that means the most to you.

Psalm 8 _____

Psalm 66:1-4 _____

Psalm 93 _____

Psalm 96 _____

Psalm 100 _____

Psalm 111 _____

Psalm 145 _____

Psalm 150 _____

5. Record phrases of praise from the following psalms.
Psalm 9:1-2

Psalm 47:1-2

Psalm 89:1

Psalm 104:1

6. The inhabitants of heaven continually praise the Lord. Record some phrases of the song of praise in each of the following verses.

The four living creatures: Revelation 4:8

The twenty-four elders: Revelation 4:11

The angels: Revelation 5:12

The victorious believers: Revelation 15:3-4

The multitude: Revelation 19:6-7

7. On a separate sheet of paper, write a brief hymn of praise to the Lord.

*Praise the LORD. How good it is to sing praises to our God, how pleasant and fitting to praise him!* (Psalm 147:1).
*Let everything that has breath praise the LORD. Praise the LORD* (Psalm 150:6).

*Written by Helen Silvey*

Quote Psalm 34:4 from memory, and be prepared to say it aloud with your group.

**Bible Study Series**

# Isaiah

**LESSON 5**

■ A Study of Isaiah, Chapters 13—24

---

*Lesson 5 starts a section of scriptures, Isaiah 13—23, that are prophecies against nine nations and Jerusalem. These prophecies have been called "oracles" or "burdens," for they tell of the coming judgment. The basic theme is God's sovereignty, for He rules the nations. Man proposes, but God disposes. Here are some simple guidelines to refer back to as these scriptures are studied.*

## DAY ONE

# Broom of Destruction

**Read Isaiah 13 and 14:22-32.**
- Babylon represents idolatry and false religions.
- Philistia represents once-true religion that no longer believes what it did believe—apostate religion.
- Moab represents formal religion but denies the power thereof.
- Damascus represents compromise.
- Cush (Ethiopia) represents missions.
- Egypt represents the world.
- Assyria represents luxury and antagonism toward God's people.
- Edom represents flesh.
- Jerusalem represents politics instead of religion.
- Tyre represents commercialism.

1. The last phrase of Isaiah 13:3 tells us the reason God has commanded His "holy ones." What is the reason?

2. Record the last phrase of verse 5, which tells us why His wrath is to be executed.

3. What will the reaction of people be on the day of the Lord's judgment? Read Isaiah 13:7-8.

4. What will be the result of this judgment to people, as told in verses 12, 15, and 16?

5. What will happen to the earth on the day of the Lord's judgment? See Isaiah 13:9-10, 13.

6. What is the purpose of this judgment, as told to us in verse 11?

7. Who will overthrow Babylon?

---

## MEMORY CHALLENGE

# Psalm 34:5

*Those who look to him are radiant;
their faces are never covered with shame.*

8. What will be the result of Babylon's overthrow, as described in Isaiah 13:20-22?

9. The end of this story is told in Revelation 18. Scan this chapter, and jot some notes or write a summary below.

10. Summarize Isaiah 14:22-23. Be sure to look for the phrase from today's title, "Broom of Destruction."

Can you remember when a popular theme for political campaigns was "Sweep out the old—bring in the new"? For some it evoked a mental picture of a granny with a gray bun and glasses, wearing an apron over a dress, out on the front sidewalk taking a broom after a cat walking through her flowerbeds. She'd sweep it away! We were supposed to do the same with our vote against corrupt politicians who were in office.

God has a universe-size broom, and when He sweeps away the evil, there is destruction. Isaiah begins to relate this to us in Isaiah 13.

Babylon always represents evil in the Bible. Babylon had its birth at the Tower of Babel. If man could be united against God, then God would divide them. Babylon was always united in rebellion against God, but that does not mean He could not use them.

When Isaiah prophesied about Babylon, it was a small, insignificant place in the world. Under Nebuchadnezzar, during Daniel's day, Babylon became a great nation. In Isaiah's day it was the chief province of Assyria, and Sargon was its leader.

According to W. E. Vine, there are four points of God's divine dealing with His chosen people, Israel. (The term "Israel" encompasses both Israel and Judah. In Isaiah's day the two nations were divided into the Northern Kingdom and Southern Kingdom but were often still referred to simply as Israel.) First, the rebellion of the people caused God to use Gentile nations to rebuke and chastise them. Second, the cruelty and abuse of power given these Gentile nations brought judgment on them. Third, His covenant and mercy will bring restoration to His people. Finally, they (Israel) will bless peoples of the world, or the Gentile nations.

So the destruction of Babylon relates to the election of Israel. Israel was rejected as God's chosen people when Babylon overran Judah, which was after Isaiah's time. Babylon's prophecy of destruction means God has once again chosen Israel. He will have mercy on Jacob, and Israel will be elected. The broom of destruction will sweep Babylon out of power. The former taskmasters will be servants and slaves, and the captors will now be the captives. The hardship of the captivity will be replaced by the song of triumph. The fall of Babylon means God has compassion on Israel again.

The broom of destruction is described well in Isaiah 13. God makes it clear how complete it will be. Keeping in mind that Babylon represents not only itself as a nation but also evil in general, we see that the broom of destruction has significance for our day. Evil will be swept away in God's timing, but *If my people, who are called by my name, will humble themselves and pray and seek my face and turn from their wicked ways, then will I hear from heaven and will forgive their sin and will heal their land* (2 Chronicles 7:14).

# Boldly "I Will"

**Read Isaiah 14:1-21.**

1. Israel's taunt is against whom? (verse 4)

2. As a review, what is Babylon symbolic of?

3. Summarize Isaiah 14:12. To whom are these verses referring?

4. Summarize Revelation 12:7-9 for further help with the answer to question 3.

5. Most commentators believe Isaiah 14:12-21 is speaking of Satan. What are Satan's five "I will's" in these verses?

6. The concept of sin may be addressed in several ways. One definition is "outward action that does not yield obedience to the will of God" *(New Westminster Dictionary of the Bible)*. How is Satan's "I will" different from this?

7. Some important concepts regarding sin (Satan's purpose) and righteousness (Christ's purpose) are found in 1 John 3:7-8. Summarize these verses.

Sin is setting our will over God's will, and that's what Satan is all about. Even in heaven he could not be obedient but wanted his own way. He picked Babylon as his kingdom on earth, and every representation of it in the Bible symbolizes Satan's power on earth. In the present day we have only to look around us to know Satan's power is real. He does indeed rule much of the earth. In the temptation of Jesus in the wilderness, the devil showed Him all the kingdoms of the world and said to Him, *I will give you all their authority and splendor, for it has been given to me* (Luke 4:6). Satan is consumed with his own plans. He cares nothing for coming under God's authority. The two most important words in his vocabulary are "I will."

Pride was Satan and Babylon's downfall. The *Guideposts Family Concordance* defines pride as "a conceited sense of one's superiority." It's the idea that I'm as special as God. Therefore, I control my life and how I appear to others—"I will."

> You had the seal of perfection,
> Full of wisdom and perfect in beauty.
> You were in Eden, the garden of God;
> Every precious stone was your covering. . . .
> You were the anointed cherub who covers,
> And I placed you there.
> You were on the holy mountain of God;
> You walked in the midst of the stones of fire.
> You were blameless in your ways
> From the day you were created
> Until unrighteousness was found in you.
> By the abundance of your trade
> You were internally filled with violence,
> And you sinned;
> Therefore I have cast you as profane
> From the mountain of God.
> And I have destroyed you, O covering cherub,
> From the midst of the stones of fire.
> Your heart was lifted up because of your beauty;
> You corrupted your wisdom by reason of your splendor.
> I cast you to the ground;
> I put you before kings,
> That they may see you.
> By the multitude of your iniquities,
> In the unrighteousness of your trade
> You profaned your sanctuaries.
> Therefore I have brought fire from the midst of you;
> It has consumed you,
> And I have turned you to ashes on the earth
> In the eyes of all who see you.
> All who know you among the peoples
> Are appalled at you;
> You have become terrified
> And you will cease to be forever.
> (Ezekiel 28:12-19, NASB)

This is a description of Satan.

One simple concept to glean from today's study is to beware of boldly saying, "I will." If we choose to live a life surrendered to God, we must do His bidding, His will, and follow His laws and ways. A simple way to keep check on ourselves is to ask the Holy Spirit to warn us when in our hearts, words, or actions we are living out "I will." He has promised to make us aware if we truly want to follow Him. Pause now and request the Holy Spirit to be your accountability partner in refusing to follow "I will."

## MEMORY CHALLENGE

We have just looked at the fall of Satan. Whose faces do you think the memory verse is saying shall never be ashamed?

# Barefoot and Bald

**Read Isaiah 15—20.**

1. Match the topic with the chapter:

   a. The Lord is riding on a          Isaiah 15
      swift cloud and is about to
      come to Egypt.

   b. Damascus will become a          Isaiah 16
      fallen ruin.

   c. Message to Cush (Ethiopia)      Isaiah 17

   d. In a night Moab is destroyed.   Isaiah 18

   e. The citizens of Egypt and       Isaiah 19
      Cush will be led away
      barefoot and naked.

   f. Moab shall wail for its         Isaiah 20
      devastation.

2. What is the condition of the people in Moab as described in Isaiah 15:2 and Jeremiah 48:37?

3. As a sign and token against Egypt and Cush, how did
   Isaiah appear for three years, according to Isaiah 20:3?

4. Who are these people who are described as barefoot,
   bald, and naked?

The six chapters studied for today are prophecies and
judgments on several nations or cities. To understand
what is happening in Isaiah's culture and world, some basic understanding of these prophecies would be helpful.

In Isaiah 15—16, Moab is suddenly overrun. The refugees
fleeing Moab clog the roads, carrying pitifully few posses-

sions and crying as they stumble along. Their tongues swell
from lack of water, for the streams are dried up or full of
blood from battle. After arriving in Edom, the Moabite fugi-
tives send a tribute to the king of Judah begging for refuge
until the crisis is over and the enemy is gone. The tribute is
lambs, meaning Moab now recognizes the God of Israel. But
the plea is rejected due to Moab's reputation. She has been
arrogant and begs only to get her way. Judah believes she is
insincere, so the sad lament continues.

Moab was the nation that came from Lot and his incestu-
ous relationship with his elder daughter. They were neighbors with God's people but were never a part. Isaiah
seemed to have pity on Moab that he did not show on other nations. Maybe he was able to sense God's heart about
these people.

In Isaiah 17 Israel and Damascus were linked to protect
themselves against Assyria. Judah was asking Assyria for
aid against the Israel-Damascus coalition, which was
threatening Judah from the north. Isaiah disagreed with
this and felt instead that their defense should be God. Judah needed to quit trusting in their own policies and trust
in God. Isaiah knew Israel's trust was misplaced and that
this would be shown if Damascus, whom they relied upon
for their defense, was destroyed. Judgment was pronounced against Israel, especially Ephraim, because they
allied themselves with Damascus against Judah. Only a
remnant would be left who would turn steadfastly to God
and abandon idolatry.

In Isaiah 19 Yahweh comes to Egypt riding on a cloud. The
gods of Egypt tremble at His presence and begin to consult their diviners and idols. The leaders of Egypt are
scared, and the nation is in turmoil. With so many gods in
their country, there is no unity. Disaster strikes as the Nile
dries up, vegetation dies, and no fish are left in the river. If
Egypt were wise, she could figure this out, but she isn't.

Isaiah's three years of nakedness, described in Isaiah 20,
was to show the desolation of Egypt. Israel therefore
could not count on Egypt and should not make an alliance
with her. Isaiah's message was that no help would come
from Egypt or Cush (Ethiopia) against Assyria. If the people of Judah trusted in Egypt, they would end up like the
Egyptians—barefoot and naked—for they would be captives and would be deported. But in the end God would
treat Egypt as His own people. Free trade between her and
Assyria would show forgiveness and healing, and they
would unite to serve the Lord. Israel would be a full partner with them.

Isaiah dressed for three years as a captive in obedience to
the Lord. He was demonstrating visually for the people
what their fate would be. If they chose to follow their own
will and disobey the Lord, their captivity to a foreign nation would be the result.

We, too, make choices about captivity. When we choose to follow our own will, including our desires, ambitions, ideas, and plans, we disobey God. Our heart belongs to something else, and in the end it will hold us captive. Have you ever known someone who was going to work hard, make lots of money for a few years, and then back off? Did it happen, or did he or she become captive to the work and money? Have you known someone who was just going to sneak a peek at a *Playboy* or an X-rated movie and soon was held captive to pornography? What about a woman who was just going to strictly diet and to exercise three hours a day until she was a size 3? Did it quit there, or was she soon in the throes of an eating disorder? Must the questions go on, or is it evident that what we choose to do outside of God's will and laws will lead us to captivity? Are we all slaves to something, whether it's good or evil? Are we slaves to Christ? Are we His captives?

Isaiah tried to warn these nations as God gave him the prophecies. They could choose freedom, or they could choose captivity. What holds you captive? Close this day's study with an honest, heart-searching moment, asking God to show you if you are captive to anything other than Christ. He does not want you to be barefoot, bald, and naked.

## MEMORY CHALLENGE

Psalm 25:3 is a cross reference to the memory challenge. It also refers to today's theme. Record it here.

## DAY FOUR

# Beckoning Mirage

**Read Isaiah 21.**

1. Isaiah 21:1 in the *New American Standard Bible* starts off with *The oracle concerning the wilderness of the sea.* This is a strange and contradictory phrase, a paradox. John saw a vision of something similar with the great harlot. Read Revelation 17:1-3, and write the location of the harlot and what she was sitting on according to verse 1.

2. This oracle is concerning Babylon, which was already dealt with in the oracles in chapters 13—14. Either Isaiah sees Babylon as a desert in the middle of the sea, or a sea in the middle of a desert. The latter is like walking down a hot highway in the middle of August and seeing a pool of water on the blacktop ahead. As you get closer, you realize it's not real—it's just a mirage. How do you think Babylon is a beckoning mirage?

3. Shadrach, Meshach, and Abednego realized Babylon was just a mirage. How did they respond to it? Record Daniel 3:18.

4. Mary realized that the things representing Babylon are a beckoning mirage to us all. Summarize the story of Mary and Martha in Luke 10:38-42. What was Mary's decision in this story?

5. Look up Luke 12:29-31. Personalize verse 31.

Babylon represents wealth, power, success, pleasure, and evil. The attraction to Babylon is great, for all that the world holds dear is there. The human side of us wants comfort, fun, relaxation, and happiness—none of which is bad. But when these things become our focus, they then take the place of God, who is to be No. 1 in our lives. Competition develops in our heart for pleasure or God. The conflict begins, and we war with ourselves. Who will win out?

This is the lure of Babylon. Shadrach, Meshach and Abednego saw it but stood firm in following their God. In a less dramatic and obvious way, Martha fell prey to choosing what looked important (preparing refreshment for her guests) but was insignificant compared to sitting at the feet of Jesus, worshiping, and learning.

For most of us this is a daily struggle. It may feel good to get to work early to have a jump on the day or to jog first thing in the morning. But maybe what's most vital is to focus first on God and His Word and His guidance for that day. What looks most important to us from the world's point of view isn't what God would classify as most important.

Isn't this what a mirage is? What we see with our eye is not in reality there. Our eyes are tricking us. All of Babylon's glitz fools us into thinking that this is it: fun, power, and wealth are what we want above all else, but such a life has no substance. Just as we finally get to that pool in the desert, we realize there is no water. The pool is not real—it was not what it appeared and therefore will not satisfy.

Mary was seeking the Kingdom first and recognized what was most important. Martha was caught in the mirage of tasks or busyness. What is really most important?

Darwin had a beautiful baritone voice and was on his way to success in opera when the Lord called him into the music ministry. The idea that he would be happy in opera, despite the fact that God had called him into music ministry, was a mirage. He obeyed and found fulfillment in life. Jim had a great arm and was headed to the major leagues to pitch. But God put His hand on him to be a minister. Jim obeyed, avoiding what looked to other people like the thing to do. He never regretted his decision, for he chose what was most important. But for most of us, the decisions are not that big or sweeping in our lives. It's more the daily choices—devotions or jogging. We daily choose what is most important.

What the world paints as valuable or important is often a mirage. It beckons us. *But seek ye first the kingdom of God, and his righteousness; and all these things shall be added unto you* (Matthew 6:33, KJV).

## MEMORY CHALLENGE

Write out the memory verse below.

## DAY FIVE

# Believer's Defense

**Read Isaiah 22.**

1.  Isaiah 22 is divided into two sections. The first is regarding the city of Jerusalem, or "the Valley of Vision." Summarize verses 1-14.

2.  The theme of the above verses is important. If you did not include it in your summary, do so now. Also look up Jeremiah 21:13 to confirm this theme.

3.  Record Isaiah 22:11.

4.  What do you believe this section of Scripture is teaching a nation, a group of people, or an individual about his or her defense? What is a "believer's defense"?

5.  Record the following scriptures regarding our defense.

    2 Kings 19:34

    Zechariah 9:15 (first phrase)

6.  David knew the Lord as his defense. Record the following Psalms. Claim them as your own.

    Psalm 7:10

    Psalm 62:2

    Psalm 94:22

The oracle of Jerusalem, or the Valley of Vision, was placed in the middle of the prophecies of foreign nations, because one of Judah's great sins was foreign alliance. God's command was to rely on Him alone as the nation's defense. Instead, the people forgot God and chose to rely on their own strategies. They rejoiced when the army was cut down in battle, because so far Jerusalem was safe. Isaiah knew they should be humbling themselves before God, fasting, and calling on His name. But they were feasting and saying, *Let us eat and drink . . . for tomorrow we die!* (Isaiah 22:13). What a flippant attitude! They thought nothing about God and His judgment. We see similar behavior in our culture.

Shebna was the chamberlain over the king's household. He had an elaborate tomb made for himself in which to be buried in honor. He quite likely was not a trustworthy person, and some has been written about the possibility of Shebna's misappropriation of funds. He most likely pushed the alliance with Egypt. Isaiah stated that God had ordained that Shebna be removed from office. He would not be buried in his prestigious tomb, for he would be carried away into a foreign country, where he would die.

Eliakim would take Shebna's place, because God would put him there *like a peg into a firm place* (verse 23). But he was warned of the dangers of high office. For him the danger was including too much of family in his duties, and the well-driven peg would give way.

God said of Eliakim, *What he opens no one can shut, and what he shuts no one can open* (verse 22). This phrase is also found in Revelation 3:7. What God decides and ordains no one can change. What He opens no one can shut, for God has complete power. What He shuts no one can open, for He has no adversary as strong as He.

God holds even the nations of the world in His hands. He is their defense. If they disobey Him, their human defenses of horses, chariots, city walls, armies—or, in our day, warheads, nuclear bombs, or invisible-to-radar planes—will make no difference. What He opens or shuts is the way it is. Humanity is no match for God.

Many years have passed since Isaiah's day. But we serve an unchanging God, and a thousand years in our world is like a day to Him. Our defense is still God, whether we are speaking politically of our nation, of a group of people such as Jews or Christians, or individually. Our plans are vain compared to God's. He opens, He shuts, and He defends. The believer's defense is alliance to God and His wonderful ways.

## MEMORY CHALLENGE

Why were the people radiant?

## DAY SIX

# Broken World

**Read Isaiah 23—24.**

1. The judgment against the last nation is in Isaiah 23. What nation is this? List any points that strike you personally.

2. The judgment moves from the cities and nations to the whole earth. Summarize the following verses:

   Isaiah 24:1-6

   2 Peter 3:7

3. The judgment against the nations has been fulfilled in history. However, most commentators agree that Isaiah 24 is about the judgment at the end of the world. Summarize Christ's words in Luke 21:25-36. Then record Luke 21:33.

4. If earthly things will pass away but the words of Christ are eternal, wouldn't we do well to place more credence in His words than anything? Our broken worlds can be restored through the healing power of His words. Record some of these words in the scriptures below.

   Matthew 11:28

   John 8:11 (second half)

   John 16:33

5.  Is there any way that your world is broken? The good news of brokenness is God's restoration. Use the following space to write a prayer that's on your heart.

Debra grew up in a very broken world. Her mother married several times, always to an abusive husband. The family lived in poverty and violence. At times her mother simply could not cope with the six kids and would turn them over to an orphanage or foster care. Life was unsettled, unpredictable, and unfair.

It's no wonder that Debra continued in the same lifestyle as an adult. She became involved with illegal drugs, alcohol, shoplifting, promiscuity, and abusive men. She had no power to break this pattern, for she knew no other way. She was hardworking and loved her two boys but often could not be the mother to them she desired because her own coping skills were so poor. Two marriages failed, and then a back injury caused her to be unable to work.

In Debra's late 30s a friend introduced her to Christ. She became involved in a church strong on Bible study, worship, and fellowship. She began to see a new way and took baby steps to change her life. She waged battle on her drinking, illegal drugs, shoplifting, and promiscuity—and eventually conquered them. Her relationship with her grown boys improved, and her life became more stable with church activities and the running of a home.

Debra's life was still a struggle as she suffered from post-traumatic stress disorder. She occasionally suffered flashbacks, days when healthy functioning was a real challenge, and incredible back pain. When she had contact with the family she grew up in, it could be an emotional setback. But God is in the business of repairing broken worlds. Debra's restoration is a process, and her broken world is in repair.

Today's scripture reports the judgment of the last nation studied in this section, Tyre, and also speaks of that day of judgment when the world will be burned up with fire. Yet God promises us a new heaven and a new earth, as recorded in Revelation 21—22. He also promises restoration to our personal broken worlds here on earth if we will turn to Him. As we read in 1 John 1:9, *If we confess our sins, He is faithful and just and will forgive us our sins and purify us from all unrighteousness.* As we turn to Him,

the process of restoration begins. God always finishes what He starts. Paul wrote in Philippians 1:6, *I am confident of this very thing, that He who began a good work in you will perfect it until the day of Christ Jesus* (NASB).

Debra's story is not unique. What God did for her He will do for you too. You must simply ask Him to restore your broken world. Confess now, and allow Him to start the process.

*Written by Linda Shaw*

## MEMORY CHALLENGE

Fill in the blanks:

*I will _____ the Lord at all _____;
his _____ will always be on my _____.*

*My soul will _____ in the Lord; let the
_____ hear and _____.*

*_____ the Lord with me; let us _____ his
name _____.*

*I sought the _____, and he _____ me; he
_____ me from all my _____.*

*Those who look to _____ are _____; their
_____ are never covered with _____.*

Psalm 34:1-5

# Isaiah

**LESSON 6**

## DAY ONE

# Perfect Faithfulness

**Read Isaiah 25:1-8.**

1. Personalize Isaiah 25:1.

2. Isaiah 25:4 gives us four pictures of God's protection. List these.

   1.

   2.

   3.

   4.

3. Isaiah 25:6-8 promises five actions God Almighty will take on our behalf. What are they?

   1.

   2.

   3.

   4.

   5.

4. Do we believe God will be faithful to bring about what He has promised? Give a definition of "faithful," using a dictionary or Bible concordance.

5. What would God's perfect faithfulness look like? Record or summarize the following verses.

   Deuteronomy 7:9

   1 Kings 8:20 (first phrase)

   1 Corinthians 1:9

   2 Thessalonians 3:3

   2 Timothy 2:13

   Hebrews 10:23

   1 John 1:9

## MEMORY CHALLENGE

# Psalm 34:6

*This poor man called, and the LORD heard him; he saved him out of all his troubles.*

6. God's perfect faithfulness is portrayed in Psalm 89:1-18, 33. Read and meditate on this psalm, noting some key points about God's faithfulness.

In this lesson we will study Isaiah 25—27. These chapters contain the songs of the redeemed and tell of God's triumph on earth in the future. The song studied today is one of thanksgiving. God is given praise and honor in verse 1 and then hails the fall of an enemy city in verse 2. This is symbolic of God's final victory, as many commentators believe Isaiah 25 tells of the triumph after the Tribulation period in God's millennium kingdom. At that point in history, *strong peoples* (Isaiah 25:3) will honor God. These are people who in the past did not give Him reverence or service. But God has silenced their rebellion and in the meantime given His people protection.

Now God offers His people freedoms. Ross E. Price in the *Beacon Bible Commentary* volume on Isaiah through Daniel states these four freedoms. First is freedom from hunger and thirst (verse 6). Second is freedom from ignorance, because the veil that keeps us from seeing God clearly will be lifted (verse 7). Our eyes will be opened. We will see and understand. Third, death and sorrow will pass away (verse 8), giving us glorious freedom. Last, there will be freedom from the curse, that is, the reproach of the people will be taken away.

Isaiah 25 reveals God's faithfulness to His people even when times appear somewhat hopeless. God cannot be anything but himself, which is faithful. He is always trustworthy and can be relied upon to keep His covenants and promises without fail. God cannot go back on His Word. Even when we disappoint our Lord and break faith and do not follow His commands, His faithfulness is perfect.

Lucinda Thomas had been married to Roy for 28 years when it was discovered he had a brain tumor. This is her testimony less than two years later.

I stand in awe of how the Holy Spirit is able to minister to me in my day-to-day existence. Over and over again in my life, God has proven himself *faithful!* When I needed strength to continue in my marriage—God gave it. When I needed courage to confront my husband or son—He provided it. When I've needed compassion or a loving gentle spirit—God has given it to me!

And when I faced Roy's death—God was my Comforter! What more could I ask than for God to be *faithful?* Several times in my marriage the world would have said, "Call it quits—throw in the towel!"

But I had a covenant with the Father—His promise to me was "A healed Roy is worth waiting for!" In our marriage, that promise was proven true. As I sat with Roy during his one-month fight with cancer, I could truthfully say, "I have no regrets!" Each challenge we had faced was another avenue for God to show us His *faithfulness.*

As I continue my walk with the Lord in this new chapter of my life, I do not fear, for I know God is faithful to meet each new need. I lift praises to the Father!

*Because of the LORD's great love we are not consumed, for his compassions never fail. They are new every morning; great is your faithfulness* (Lamentations 3:22-23).

*Great is Thy faithfulness, O God, my Father;*
*There is no shadow of turning with Thee.*
*Thou changest not; Thy compassions, they fail not.*
*As Thou has been Thou forever wilt be.*

*Great is Thy faithfulness! Great is Thy faithfulness!*
*Morning by morning new mercies I see.*
*All I have needed Thy hand hath provided.*
*Great is Thy faithfulness, Lord, unto me!*

—Thomas O. Chisholm

## DAY TWO

# Patiently Waiting

**Read Isaiah 25:9-12.**

1. Record Psalm 37:7.

*The Message* has a similar verse in Revelation 14: *Meanwhile, the saints stand passionately patient, keeping God's commands, staying faithful to Jesus* (verse 12).

2. Find a translation of Isaiah 25:9 that uses the word "waited." Record the verse here. (Refer to NASB, TLB, KJV, NKJV, RSV.)

3. Define "patience," using a Bible concordance or dictionary.

4. Record Psalm 40:1.

5. Record or summarize the following verses regarding patiently waiting.

   Psalm 27:14

   Psalm 37:34 (first phrase)

   Psalm 130:5

   Lamentations 3:24-26

   Hosea 12:6

6. Reread the above scriptures, and summarize what you think you have learned about waiting.

7. Record the great promise about waiting given us in the latter portion of Habakkuk 2:3.

Moab is a symbol of all who reject and fight against God. In today's passage, Judah is promised that Moab will be trodden down. Mount Zion, the symbol of God's blessings to His people, will have the Lord's hand resting on it. The God for whom the people have waited to save them from their enemies will deliver, and they will know the joy of His salvation.

Why does God sometimes make us wait? In a society of instant gratification, we're used to having what we want and having it now. What is the value of waiting? Simply, waiting develops patience.

Patience helps us remain calm when the timing is not to our liking. It allows us to be mature and not act like a spoiled child who isn't getting his or her way. Patience permits us to deal with other people who are irritating or working at a slower pace than we are. When problems arise, it gives us the endurance to deal with them until they are solved. We all know that in some cases this may be years. Patience gives us the strength to persevere.

*Dear brothers, is your life full of difficulties and temptations? Then be happy, for when the way is rough, your patience has a chance to grow. So let it grow, and don't try to squirm out of your problems. For when your patience is finally in full bloom, then you will be ready for anything, strong in character, full and complete* (James 1:2-4, TLB).

The scripture from Habakkuk 2:3, used by Wisdom of the Word as the "God Can!" theme, reminds us that waiting is part of God's plan. He knows when the timing is perfect. If answers arrive too soon, we don't develop the strength of character to be ready in difficult times. We don't know the heightened joy of a request for which we have waited. We may even change how God's perfect plan fits together if the timing is wrong. While we wait, we learn to trust that God is in control, and His beautiful plan will fit together in the right time.

That's easier said than done! All of us have problems at points in our lives when we feel we can't live with the pressures of another day. Then we are asked to wait, to be patient! But God knows that character building is what gives us confidence in ourselves through Him to cope with life. If He never has a chance to develop our character, then we will truly be vulnerable to the hard times. Then we may fall. Patience can be God's protection of His children.

As a little girl I heard my mother talk about her father, who was an alcoholic. My mother was saved in her teens through the influence of an aunt. At that point she began to pray for her father, who was separated from the family and living in another place. His life had been difficult because of alcohol, and he married several times before he found himself living on the streets as a drunk. But one night he wandered into a rescue mission and was saved. From there he turned his life around. Eventually he remarried and raised two foster children as his own. He remained faithful to the Lord throughout his life.

My mother talked about how she prayed for him for 25 years before he was saved. I imagine at times she felt it was pretty hopeless. But she was patient, and in God's timing her father was saved. How that must have increased her faith!

Patience has a purpose. It is not a cruel trick of the Creator to make our life more taxing. Actually, its purpose is to make us strong in the Lord, able to endure, ready for any difficulty. Our faith is both tested and developed as we wait. In today's passage Judah is told to wait—to be patient that God would save them. He promises us the same. *Those who wait for the LORD will gain new strength; they will mount up with wings like eagles, they will run and not get tired, they will walk and not become weary* (Isaiah 40:31, NASB).

## MEMORY CHALLENGE

What happened to the poor man when he called?

# Perfect Peace

**Read Isaiah 26:1-6.**

1. In that day why will Judah have a strong city?

2. For whom will the gates be opened?

3. Who will God keep in perfect peace, and why?

4. What does the Bible teach us about peace? Record or summarize the following scriptures.

   Psalm 29:11

   Psalm 85:10

   Psalm 119:165

   Romans 5:1

   Philippians 4:7

5. What does trust have to do with our peace? Record Romans 15:13.

6. What are your ideas about how we can keep our minds steadfast so He will keep us in perfect peace?

In a hustle-bustle, chaotic, crazy world, could there really be such a thing as personal peace? If your life is in turmoil even as you read this, you may have laughed or sighed and said, "Yeah, right." Jeremiah said, *Ah, Sovereign LORD, how completely you have deceived this people and Jerusalem by saying, "You will have peace," when the sword is at our throats* (Jeremiah 4:10). Know how he felt? But God has promised peace to His people—not just national peace, but personal peace. *Though the mountains be shaken and the hills be removed, yet my unfailing love for you will not be shaken nor my covenant of peace be removed* (Isaiah 54:10).

Remember the once-popular song "I Never Promised You a Rose Garden"? When circumstances are not going well, I often repeat that title to myself. It's true even for us as God's children. He does not promise us roses all the time. Roses have thorns, and so does life. When Adam and Eve made a sinful choice in the Garden of Eden, they were given some consequences, such as pain in childbirth and soil that was hard to till. We still live with that and all the other ramifications of the fall. There are plenty of difficulties in this life, and just because we are Christians does not mean we will escape them. Jesus stated, *I have told you these things, so that in me you may have peace. In this world you will have trouble. But take heart! I have overcome the world* (John 16:33).

Yes, we will have trouble. God has told us that in His Word. But let's admit it—often as Christians we are hurt, disappointed, and mad when we have trouble, because we feel God should protect us from that. I'm sure He does protect us on many occasions, but not always. What God does promise us is peace. According to John 16:33, Christ teaches us how to have peace through troubles.

How? Let's look at these verses from today's scriptures: *You will keep in perfect peace him whose mind is steadfast, because he trusts in you. Trust in the LORD forever, for the LORD, the LORD, is the Rock eternal* (Isaiah 26:3-4). When we look at circumstances, our emotions go up and down. But when we look at God, the Rock eternal, we remain steadfast. He is in control. All circumstances are within His power. Our job is to be steadfast in Him and continue to trust. Then He promises us peace in the midst of our troubles.

How easy it is to look at the circumstances because, truthfully, most would require miracles! Humanly we look at the impossibilities and begin to fear. That's why we must not look at the circumstances, but at God. Our steadfast focus must remain on Him, and we must obey Him. How many of today's scriptures relate to peace coming from righteousness, faith, trust, or loving the Law? It seems that God's ways also bring peace. Focusing on Him is one of the keys to a steadfast mind.

This steadfast mind that continues to trust in God is the key to peace. *The fruit of righteousness will be peace; the effect of righteousness will be quietness and confidence forever. My people will live in peaceful dwelling places, in secure homes, in the undisturbed places of rest* (Isaiah 32:17-18).

According to *Vine's Expository Commentary on Isaiah,*

> This is to be enjoyed at all times by those who, instead of being overcome by difficulties or by yielding to the pressure of spiritual foes and human antagonism, put their trust in the Lord, staying their mind upon Him. The peace possessed is not the outcome of mere self-determination, it is ministered by the keeping power of the Lord Himself. It is that peace which essentially characterized Christ, and of which he said, "Peace I leave with you, My peace I give unto you."[1]

Peace—His perfect peace. Keep your mind steadfast on Him.

> *"Thou wilt keep him in perfect peace,*
> *Whose mind is stayed on Thee."*
> *When the shadows come and darkness falls,*
> *He giveth inward peace.*
> *O He is the only perfect Resting Place!*
> *He giveth perfect peace.*
> *"Thou wilt keep him in perfect peace,*
> *Whose mind is stayed on Thee."*
>
> Vivian A. Kretz

## MEMORY CHALLENGE

How does today's lesson relate to this week's memory challenge?

# Passion for God

**Read Isaiah 26:7-19.**

1. What phrases in Isaiah 26:8-9 show the prophet's passion for God?

2. Read the following scriptures and lift out the phrases that show a passion for God.

   2 Chronicles 31:20-21

   Psalm 63:1

   Jeremiah 29:13

3. Personalize Psalm 42:1-2.

4. Being passionate for God seems to relate to seeking His face. Summarize these scriptures.

   Deuteronomy 4:29

   1 Chronicles 16:11

   Isaiah 55:6

5. How do you personally seek God's face? List some ways, and share with your group if you're comfortable doing so. Then ask the Lord what other ways He may want you to use to stay passionate for Him.

Today's passage of scripture is called "a prayer of entreaty and trust," or "the song of the soul's desire." The previous section, which we studied yesterday, reminded us that if the people trust the Lord and steadfastly keep their minds on Him, He will keep their nation secure and their minds in perfect peace. Today's section begins, *The path of the righteous is level* (verse 7) and goes on to promise that Israel will be enlarged. This means God's people will increase.

Israel has labored like a woman giving birth, but nothing has come of her pain and suffering. She has produced no fruit. But through the resurrection of the righteous, God will bring the dead alive, and they will sing for joy. Immortality is revealed here, telling us that God defeats death. But all this is dependent on the people *walking in the way of [God's] laws* (verse 8) and waiting for Him. Then the earth will be judged, and *the people of the world [will] learn righteousness* (verse 9). They must be passionate for God for His promises to be fulfilled.

Frank Minirth is a Christian psychiatrist who has been a pioneer in his field integrating spiritual principles with the chemical illnesses of the brain. He is the founder of the Minirth Christian Program at Green Oaks Hospital in Dallas and an adjunct professor at Dallas Theological Seminary. He has coauthored over 50 books and cohosts a national radio and television program. In a recent issue of *Christian Counseling Today* magazine, Dr. Minirth spoke of his passion for Christ:

> I am in love with Christ. I really am. I love Christ. He is my best friend. . . . He gave me a vision and reason to live. I'm mission driven by a love for Christ. . . . I'm looking for any dimension where I can share Christ and the hope we have in Him. . . . I think I will want to keep emphasizing Christ. . . . What makes us unique is Jesus Christ. I will push real hard always to keep Jesus Christ in my mind. . . . What do I do spiritually? I spend time with Christ.[1]

Can you hear the passion in his interview? His life's work, his drive, his mission in life all come from his passion for God. This is what Isaiah was saying. Passion is the key. Seek His face. Pray for passion.

## MEMORY CHALLENGE

Fill in the blanks:

*This poor man _____, and the LORD _____ him; He _____ him out of all his _____.*

Psalm 34:6

# Punish Leviathan

**Read Isaiah 26:20-21 and 27:1.**

1. Summarize Isaiah 26:20-21.

2. There are three things the Lord will punish with the sword. What are they?

3. Look up Psalm 74:14, which refers to Leviathan. Summarize and then make a guess as to who Leviathan is.

4. Isaiah 26:21 refers to prophecy that remains to be fulfilled. This is also found in Revelation 19. Isaiah 27:1 also refers to unfulfilled prophecy that is explained more in Revelation 20. Read these Revelation chapters, and use the following space to make any notes.

5. Jesus tells us the doom of Satan. Summarize what Jesus says in these verses, and note the different names for Satan.

Matthew 25:41

John 12:31

There's an old Scottish belief that a "water horse" inhabits every lake in Scotland. These animals were thought to be evil spirits that lured water travelers to death by drowning. Is it any wonder that in 1933 it was declared that the beautiful long narrow lake of Loch Ness had a monster? The many sightings of this snakelike creature of monstrous size helped explain many wooden sailing vessels that were destroyed. With time the legend grew until the Loch Ness monster became world famous.

Leviathan appears in the Bible several times and is almost like a mythical monster, similar to our present-day Loch Ness monster. Who is this Leviathan who will be punished? In general terms, it is Satan or evil. As far as what type of animal it is like, apparently a dragon-like whale or alligator are the most likely. But the name had meaning in Isaiah's culture as a fearful creature.

Today's scripture begins with God's people being warned to hide until the judgment is passed. It will be terrible but brief. All foes of the righteous will be destroyed, for the blood of the slain cries out for vengeance. These verses are about punishment.

The threefold representation of Leviathan is symbolism. The gliding or piercing serpent represents the kingdom of Assyria. Babylon is the coiling or crooked serpent; the monster of the sea, or the dragon, is Egypt. This section continues to discuss the judgments of these nations that choose to follow evil instead of God.

Isn't it interesting that whether in the Old Testament or New Testament, the same themes are repeated over and over in scripture? No other book (and this one is really 66 books rolled into one) is as consistent as the Bible is from cover to cover about themes. Once again, the theme of good overcoming evil is shown. Leviathan will be punished. God will win.

We have nothing to fear when we know the outcome. God will triumph! Punish Leviathan!

From what was the poor man saved?

# Plentiful Vineyard

**Read Isaiah 27:2-13.**

1. Summarize Isaiah's song about a fruitful vineyard found in verses 2-5.

2. *Israel will bud and blossom and fill all the world* _____ _____ (verse 6).

3. How is this song of the vineyard different from the one found in Isaiah 5:1-7?

4. God has some expectations of our lives, just like those of His vineyards. In Jeremiah 2:21 He says, *I had planted you like a choice vine of sound and reliable stock.* Record Psalm 107:37 as a response.

5. How do we make our vineyard plentiful? Summarize the following scriptures.

   Matthew 13:23

   John 15:1, 4-5

   Colossians 1:9-10

   Hebrews 13:15

6. List the fruit of the Spirit as found in Galatians 5:22-23, which makes our lives as a plentiful vineyard.

The song of Yahweh's vineyard is a promise that God will restore the earth through His people. Unlike the vineyard song in Isaiah 5, the Lord is pleased with Israel and says they will flourish like a vine and fill the whole earth with fruit. Yahweh will guard His vineyard from all harm so that no thorns or briers, which are enemies, will attack. He will protect his vineyard and trample the enemy underfoot. In regard to the earth and nation of Israel, this is a prophecy yet to come (although we saw the beginning of it with the nation of Israel's establishment in 1948).

God had told His people how to be a plentiful vineyard. All they had to do was obey. We have the same option. He has given us His Word to make it clear exactly how to be a plentiful vineyard.

Listening, abiding, praying, understanding, and praising are all part of being fruitful. As we obey and practice the principles God has given us for a Christian life, we produce fruit. We influence a friend for good, we win a soul to Christ, or we defeat evil in some fashion. Others see the fruit of the Spirit in our lives, and they are attracted to knowing what it's all about. As we point to Christ, our vineyard produces.

The joy of living is in being a fruitful vine. When we produce no fruit, there is little excitement, surprises, "God moments," or peace. We are just existing. But being a plentiful vineyard gives a reason to get up in the morning with anticipation. What is God going to do today? If we as the vine stay attached, He as the Vinedresser will produce in us! Incredible! What more fulfilling a life could we live than to be a plentiful vineyard?

*Written by Linda Shaw*

Write this week's verse from memory.

## Bible Study Series

# Isaiah

LESSON 7

■ **A Study of Isaiah, Chapters 28—31**

*Isaiah 28 begins a section of Isaiah's direct public ministry during the reign of Hezekiah. From chapters 28—33, he pronounces six woes. The first five are against Israel (the 10 northern tribes often called Ephraim in Scripture), Judah, and Jerusalem. The sixth woe is against Assyria.*

## DAY ONE

# Cornerstone

**Read Isaiah 28:1-18.**

1. Against whom is the first woe?

2. What will happen to this nation?

3. Summarize Isaiah 28:15, and then explain what you think it could possibly mean.

4. Warning is given about listening to these unwise advisers. Summarize Ezekiel 13:10-12.

5. Despite their disobedience, what will God be to His people in that day? Consult Isaiah 28:5-6.

6. What is God's promise to His people in Isaiah 28:16-17?

7. The New Testament speaks of a Cornerstone (capstone) as well. Summarize the following scriptures.

   Matthew 21:42

   Romans 9:33

   Ephesians 2:19-21

8. What is the purpose of the Cornerstone?

   Acts 4:11-12

   2 Timothy 1:9-10

## MEMORY CHALLENGE

# Psalm 34:7

*The angel of the LORD encamps around those who fear him, and he delivers them.*

9. What will happen to those who believe in the Cornerstone and those who do not, according to 1 Peter 2:4-8?

10. Record Matthew 7:24.

Many truths from this chapter are relevant to us today. First is the warning against the excess of alcohol, which in our world of addictions is very important. Drinking to excess must have become quite a problem in Israel in Isaiah's day, for he speaks out against it often. In Isaiah 28, the prophet begins by rebuking the rulers of Jerusalem who are drunkards making poor decisions for the people. He wants them to look to the north and to Samaria, whose doom is certain. Isaiah is trying to get the rulers to recognize they are making the same mistake by trusting in foreign alliances. God, not their national defense policy, is their salvation. Isaiah offends the rulers, and he in turn is enraged that they won't listen to him. So he tells them, "[If] you will not hear Yahweh's lesson spelled out in plain Hebrew, it will be taught to you in Assyrian!"[1]

Second is the warning against depending on the strength of one's defense, whether it is powerful weapons, a strong army, or foreign alliances. The treaties Judah was making with Egypt were "covenants with death." This may have also been a prophetic warning for Israel in the future not to make a pact with the Antichrist. Isaiah reminds us that God is always our true defense. If we are faithful to be obedient to Him, He will protect us.

Third, Isaiah states there can be no spiritual maturity without discipline. One cannot expect to grow strong in the Lord without prayer, fasting, meditation, Bible study, and worship. J. Vernon McGee wrote, "As people lapse into apostasy in any age, it becomes increasingly difficult to impart spiritual truth."[2]

Learning spiritual truth takes discipline, like rote lessons learned as a child in elementary school. As students may sit and recite their ABC's or multiplication tables, Isaiah says, *Do and do, do and do, rule on rule, rule on rule; a little here, a little there* (verse 10). Those truths are not imparted to a soul not willing to work. Discipline brings ma-

turity. *In fact, though by this time you ought to be teachers, you need someone to teach you the elementary truths of God's word all over again. You need milk, not solid food! Anyone who lives on milk, being still an infant, is not acquainted with the teaching about righteousness. But solid food is for the mature, who by constant use have trained themselves to distinguish good from evil* (Hebrews 5:12-14).

A fourth lesson from chapter 28 is that God provides us with opportunities to learn His lessons. If we refuse the process of learning, it becomes tougher and more painful. As Isaiah warned, if you don't want it in Hebrew, it will come through that enemy (Assyria) overpowering the nation.

Isaiah is talking to the politicians, priests, and prophets who should be under the influence of God but are instead under the influence of alcohol. Therefore, they remain spiritually immature. They are Hezekiah's advisers—and although he was a godly king, he was easily led astray by poor influence.

In the midst of a tough prophecy, this passage ends with a wonderful promise. We are told of a Cornerstone on which we can build a solid foundation. This foundation, according to verse 16, has been "tested" and is "precious." One who trusts in this foundation "will never be dismayed" (put to shame). This Cornerstone is Jesus Christ.

Jehovah promised a Person who would be the Savior of the world and would be rock solid for anyone who puts his or her trust in Him. "Cornerstone" is an Egyptian word used in Scripture that denotes a hard stone suitable for carving, not easily cracked or broken. It is rock solid. Therefore, it can be used as the corner rock of a tall, heavy building and be depended upon to hold the weight of the entire structure. At Calvary, Christ held the weight of the entire world on himself when He took on our sins. He was a sure foundation—He held strong and true to His death to become our Savior. He is someone who can be trusted and depended upon to put one's faith in.

If you haven't done that, why don't you pray the following prayer? *Jesus, I know You're the only one in this world who is completely rock solid. I know I'm a sinner and that You died on the Cross for my sins. Please forgive me of my sins, and become the Cornerstone of my life. In Your name I pray. Amen.*

# Crops

**Read Isaiah 28:18-29.**

1. Today's verses tell of more judgment. Quote the last half of Isaiah 28:19 here.

2. What will happen if the people don't stop their mocking?

3. Summarize what Isaiah says about the farmer.

4. Does God sow the same in all of our lives? Use the scriptures below to help with your answer.

   Jeremiah 35:6-8

   Hosea 1:2

   Romans 12:6

5. Read Proverbs 2:1-11. Verses 2-4 is a "to do" list for allowing God to sow positively in our lives. List the results of this, given in verses 5-11.

6. If God's purpose of sowing in our lives is knowledge and wisdom about how to live our lives, then write out what we must remember. See Isaiah 28:29.

The Assyrians will come and gobble Ephraim up like "a choice bit of fruit." [1] This happened in 721 B.C. The foreign alliance with Egypt failed as Isaiah predicted, and Yahweh came—but in the form of Assyria—against Judah. Isaiah tried to tell the people there would be no rest in godless practices. Instead, they had to find out that when they lay down to rest, *the bed is too short to stretch out on, the blanket too narrow to wrap around you* (verse 20).

Then Isaiah shifts to a parable of the farmer and his crops. He asks his listeners if a farmer plows continually. Doesn't he have a pattern of plowing, sowing, and reaping? The farmer doesn't sow aimlessly, but with a purpose. Nor does he treat every crop the same, for some are threshed and some are not; some are beaten, and some are not. The farmer works his field according to what each crop needs, and the cycle of sowing and reaping emerges.

So it is with God. He does not plow His crops—us—without a purpose. He does not treat every crop alike, for we do not all need the same thing. He did not tell every family in Israel to refrain from drinking wine, as He did the Recabites. He did not tell every prophet to take a prostitute as a wife, as He did Hosea. For each of His people, His crops, there was a purpose in their individual instruction. As a farmer works his plan, so does God amid the deluge and strife of our lives. He is working out His eternal purpose.

It's easy to look at others and ask, "Why?" Why do they have it so much easier than we do? It's very likely that they don't, for we don't know others' secret sorrows and intimate problems. But the important point is that God plows in each of our lives according to His purpose. What is it we need? What is it He wants to teach us? How do we gain wisdom and knowledge? We, His crops, are marvelously and individually tended by our heavenly Farmer.

Isaiah tells Judah that they should have at least as much sense as the farmer. We should too.

## MEMORY CHALLENGE

If the rulers, politicians, priests, and prophets in Judah had believed the truth of this week's memory verse, they would not have worried about the Assyrians. Write the verse here.

## DAY THREE

# Carnal Hearts

**Read Isaiah 29:1-14.**

1. In verses 1-4, what does Isaiah tell Ariel (Jerusalem) will happen to her?

2. By what means will the Lord deliver the city?

3. Can the people understand what Isaiah is saying to them? Summarize verses 9-12.

4. Where are the people's hearts?

5. How does God want the people's hearts to be?

   1 Chronicles 29:9

   Jeremiah 24:7

   Luke 12:29-31

   2 Corinthians 4:6

6. What is the people's worship (verse 13)?

7. God can change our worship from meaningless to meaningful by changing our hearts. How does He do this? Record or summarize the following verses.

   Psalm 51:10

   Jeremiah 12:3 (first portion)

   Ezekiel 11:19 or 36:26

   Acts 16:14

Jerusalem is symbolized here as the hearth or altar of God. But she is full of drunkenness, idleness, frivolousness, and idolatries. The people have stupefied themselves spiritually until they are like men and women who are too drunk to see what they are doing. When we stupefy our moral senses, our moral compass is lost.

But this time God will deliver them from the Assyrians. He intervenes by sending a storm including thunder, lightning, wind, fire, and earthquake. He astounds the people with *wonder upon wonder* (verse 14). The people thought Egypt would save them, but of course it was God. The wise aren't so smart after all. *The wise will be put to shame; they will be dismayed and trapped. Since they have rejected the word of the LORD, what kind of wisdom do they have?* (Jeremiah 8:9). In Christ's day it was the same. Paul says in 1 Corinthians 1:18-19, *The message of the cross is foolishness to those who are perishing, but to us who are being saved it is the power of God. For it is written: 'I will destroy the wisdom of the wise; the intelligence of the intelligent I will frustrate.'* Our generation will not be saved by intelligence either, but by the cross of Christ.

The wise of Isaiah's day said traditional worship was good enough. *Their worship of me is made up only of rules taught by men* (verse 13). Jesus spoke to this in both Matthew 15:3-9 and Mark 7:6-8. In Mark 7:6-8 Jesus said, *Isaiah was right when he prophesied about you hypocrites; as it is written: "These people honor me with their lips, but their hearts are far from me. They worship me in vain; their teachings are but rules taught by men." You have let go of the commands of God and are holding on to the traditions of men.* But God cares about the condition of our hearts. Following rules may have nothing to do with how our hearts are toward God. Ezekiel 33:31 states, *My people come to you, as they usually do, and sit before you to listen to your words, but they do not put them into practice. With their mouths they express devotion, but their hearts are greedy for unjust gain.* We would say they had carnal or sinful hearts.

Our hearts need to long for God. They need to be open to what He has to say to us and be willing to be corrected when He convicts us. Our hearts are to be pure in their desire to please God and follow His commands. The condition of our hearts is what God looks for. The longing to know God, seek Him, follow Him, and fellowship with Him comes from the pure heart God desires from us. Following rules is the easy way out. Struggling to be honest with ourselves and follow the voice of the Holy Spirit is truly a heart pleasing to God.

*Above all else, guard your heart, for it is the wellspring of life* (Proverbs 4:23). How's your heart? Is it a heart of flesh—real, honest, pulsating for God? Or is it a carnal heart—a heart of stone, following only rules made by people, which may look good to others but is far from God?

## MEMORY CHALLENGE

What does the angel of the Lord do for those who fear God?

## DAY FOUR

# Crossroads

**Read Isaiah 29:15-24.**

1.  Record Jeremiah 6:16.

2.  Against whom is the third woe pronounced (through Isaiah)?

3.  Isaiah warns the people that they act as if they were equal with God (verse 16). Summarize the following scriptures regarding God's supreme authority.

    Psalm 94:7

    Jeremiah 18:1-6

4.  Isaiah then gives the people the wonderful promise of change (verses 17-24). Summarize Isaiah 35, which expands on this promise.

5.  When we stand at the crossroads, we always have a chance for change. Each choice brings a result. Record Proverbs 1:32-33.

6.  For those who follow God, there is blessing. Record the promise in Isaiah 29:24 for those who have not followed but are at the crossroads to choose God. Claim this promise for someone whose salvation you're praying for.

Isaiah's third woe is for those who think they can make plans without God's knowledge of it. Rather ridiculous, isn't it? Does the clay tell the potter what to do? Hardly. In spite of their arrogance, Isaiah promises a change when the wilderness will become a fertile valley and the desert a garden. Life will be different with these hardhearted ones then—for they will no longer be blind or deaf. They will come out of the darkness. *Those who are wayward in spirit will gain understanding; those who complain will accept instruction* (verse 24). What an incredible promise!

The times when we stand at the crossroads are often when such blessings are determined. Which way will we go? A godly choice brings blessings, although there may be hardship involved. But an ungodly choice brings unpleasant consequences into our lives.

In ancient times an enemy captured a godly king's son. With their golden prisoner they advanced on the capital of the nation. The mighty warriors of the nation had a choice: to defend the city or try to recapture the son in covert operations. They were at a crossroad. Which choice would they make? They inquired of the Lord, and He said to defend the city. Then God gave them a battle defense: stay in the city and wait to fight until He said, "Now."

As the army advanced, a grass fire started in the middle of the troops. The countryside was incredibly dry, and the fire spread rapidly. With no resources to fight it, the troops could not escape in time and were badly burned and rendered immobile, except those in the back. The fire did not spread there, and, of course, this is where the king's son was. When the fire burned out as quickly as it started, the citizens of the capital could run straight forward to the back of the troops and easily defeated those guarding the king's son. Not only was the city saved, but the son was rescued as well.

Life is full of crossroads. Sometimes the way to righteousness is not very clear. But as in the previous story, we inquire of the Lord. Day Six covers this wonderful scripture from Isaiah 30:21—*Whether you turn to the right or to the left, your ears will hear a voice behind you, saying, "This is the way; walk in it."*

At the crossroads, will we be wayward in spirit or acknowledge the Holy One of Israel?

## MEMORY CHALLENGE

Who does the angel of the Lord deliver?

## DAY FIVE

# Conned

**Read Isaiah 30:1-18 and 31:1-9.**

1. What is the fourth woe Isaiah pronounces against *the obstinate children?*

2. What did the *rebellious people* want, according to Isaiah 30:9-11?

3. What did the people rely and depend upon, according to Isaiah 30:12?

4. What is a definition of deceit? How does this fit with today's title, "Conned"?

5. We are warned against allowing ourselves to be conned. Summarize these passages.

   Jeremiah 9:8

   Romans 7:11

   1 Corinthians 3:18

   2 Timothy 3:13

6. People were willing to be deceived or "conned" when Christ came. Summarize the following scriptures.

2 Corinthians 11:3, 13-15

2 Thessalonians 2:9-12

1 John 4:1-3

7. According to Isaiah 30:15, what should be the people's salvation and strength?

Isaiah 30 tells of the fourth woe against the obstinate children of Judah who cling to this alliance with Egypt in safety against Assyria. The fifth woe in Isaiah 31 is more of the same. Isaiah tried to tell the people that Egypt was *Rahab the Do-Nothing* (30:7). In discussing the animals of the Negev, he warned that just as these animals are dangerous to humans, so the rulers of Egypt will prove to be dangerous to Judah. Then, in Isaiah 30:8, the prophet orders a written record to serve as proof when it comes true. He is trying to tell the people that God will have His way no matter what they plan.

But the people want to be conned. They want the seers to give only good visions and the prophets to tell them *pleasant things . . . illusions* (verse 10). They do not want a messenger of God to confront them with the truth. Yet Isaiah tells them that only in repentance and rest will they have salvation and that there will be no strength without quietness and trust. They are reminded that God is a God of justice and that He longs to show them compassion, but they must deal in truth.

John lived in the same town as his elderly mother, whose health seemed to be declining. He became concerned that she was not eating properly, taking her medicine correctly, and could be so forgetful that she would do unsafe things such as leave boiling food on the stove and go outside to sit. He began to fear for her safety.

John called his sister in a state far away, but she did not want to believe that her mother was not the strong, capable woman she had always been. "I'm sure she's OK," she told John. "Don't worry about it."

So John continued to do the best he could to keep an eye on his mother. But six weeks later she forgot to test the bath water before she got in the tub and severely burned herself. She was taken to the hospital in an ambulance and had to suffer through severe pain and some skin grafting. While she was there, some mental tests were administered, and it was concluded that she was no longer capable of living alone. What pain and heartache could have been avoided if John's sister had wanted to hear the truth! But she wasn't ready to admit her mother was failing, so she chose to be conned. She chose to live in denial.

The people of Judah wanted only to be told what they wanted to hear. They did not want the truth. But when we watch someone else with such a situation, we know they're asking for disaster. We often want to be conned—we want to live in denial if the circumstance affects us and is not what we want it to be. God wants us to deal with truth whether it's about His Word, His will, or the circumstances of our lives. The Scriptures warn us against false teachings or believing in deceit. Our denial of reality does not change reality; it only hides it from us.

Jesus said, *You will know the truth, and the truth will set you free* (John 8:32).

## MEMORY CHALLENGE

Fill in the blanks:

*The _____ of the LORD _____ around _____ who _____ him, and he _____ them.*

Psalm 34:7

# Contrast: Bread of Adversity, Broad Meadows

**Read Isaiah 30:19-33.**

1. What are the people of Jerusalem told in Isaiah 30:19?

2. Although they have been given *the bread of*

   _____ *and the water of* _____,
   (verse 20), the people will now see their teachers.
   Record 30:21.

3. God promises restoration. Record or summarize the
   promises given in the following scriptures.

   Psalm 71:20

   Jeremiah 31:4

   Jeremiah 33:6

4. Reread Isaiah 30:23-26. Then summarize Psalm 65:9-13.

5. What bread of adversity and water of affliction has God
   put in your life? If comfortable, share with your group
   some ways that He gave you strength to handle it.

6. Into which broad meadows has God led you? Share
   your praises with someone.

*In shady green pastures so rich and so sweet,*
   *God leads His dear children along.*
*Where the water's cool flow bathes the weary one's feet,*
   *God leads His dear children along.*

*Sometimes on the mount where the sun shines so bright,*
   *God leads His dear children along.*
*Sometimes in the valley in darkest of night,*
   *God leads His dear children along.*

*Some thro' the waters, some thro' the flood,*
   *Some thro' the fire, but all thro' the blood.*
*Some thro' great sorrow, but God gives a song*
   *In the night season and all the day long.*

—G. A. Young

The well-known hymn quoted above depicts today's theme
well. God leads us along paths that are rocky and level,
but He always leads. This is a pattern of life that's always
shifting. For weeks or years circumstances may run so
smoothly, and then a time of great difficulty comes. If we
persevere, level paths will once again emerge.

The people of Judah were experiencing the bread of adversity and the water of affliction. But notice that during
the adversity and affliction there would be bread and water. Even farther down the road they were promised broad
meadows. God promised that they would weep no more.
He promised rain and rich land and food.

When we experience the bread of adversity, how do we react spiritually? Do we continue to trust in God and believe
He will lead us back to broad meadows if we are patient
and faithful? Or do we look at the circumstances and begin to doubt that God is in control? Sometimes if we can
remind ourselves of this pattern that life goes through, it
helps us as we eat the bread of adversity.

Today's scripture shows that God will wait for His timing
and then show mercy. During tough times He will be our
Teacher and will guide us in specific ways.

Don't be deceived by the bread of adversity. It comes to all
of us and does not mean God has changed. It's part of the
pattern of life—He is still in control. Broad meadows are
just around the corner.

*Written by Linda Shaw*

## MEMORY CHALLENGE

Quote aloud this week's verse.

# Isaiah

**LESSON 8**

■ A Study of Isaiah, Chapters 32—35

---

## DAY ONE

## DAY ONE

# Reign of Righteousness

**Read Isaiah 32.**

Isaiah's prophecies of woe continue to be followed by prophecies of great blessing for the future. In this chapter, Isaiah foretells a kingdom of righteousness, peace, and prosperity. Most Bible commentators believe the complete fulfillment of this prophecy will be the millennial kingdom under the reign of the Messiah King, Jesus Christ, which will take place after the Great Tribulation.

1. How will the king reign?

   How will the rulers (princes) reign?

2. Describe what each of these rulers will be like.

3. Read Isaiah 4. What are we promised in Isaiah 4:6?

4. What will happen to the blind eyes? (32:3)

   What will happen to the deaf ears?

   What will happen to the rash mind (verse 4)?

   What will happen to the stammering tongue?

This blessed kingdom of righteousness will be under the reign of the Messiah King, Jesus Christ—King of Kings and Lord of Lords. The leaders under Him will be people of character, wisdom, and discernment. The King and His princes will not be oppressors but will provide protection, shelter, refreshment, and shade. No inequality or unfairness will exist in this kingdom.

No longer will eyes be blind to truth; neither will perception of character be confused or misinterpreted by cloudy vision. Each individual will be recognized as what he or she actually is. Fools and scoundrels will be exposed. Ears will be opened to listen willingly and obediently to the Word of God and to His instruction and guidance. The once-rash mind will have good judgment and understanding. The stammering tongue no longer will speak lies but rather will proclaim prophetic truth.

The United States endured a difficult and rancorous presidential election in November 2000, and the final outcome was not determined until several weeks after the election. As Christians, we pray for wisdom, clear sight, and guidance, but sometimes Satan continues to cloud our vision. How wonderful will be this kingdom, where everyone's vision is clear and unobstructed—and fools and scoundrels will be totally exposed.

The rulers and people of Judah during Isaiah's day were fearful and insecure, frequently besieged by enemies, turning to human alliances and impotent gods rather than trusting Almighty God. Their eyes were closed to the true

---

# Psalm 34:8

*Taste and see that the LORD is good;*
*blessed is the man who takes refuge in him.*

Source of their salvation by their fear and by their lack of trust in God. They refused to hear the clear truth of God's warnings and commands through His prophets. Instead, they listened to fools and put their trust in scoundrels. Into this darkness and despair Isaiah brought a message of light and hope to the children of God.

These promised blessings have already been fulfilled in the hearts of the followers of Jesus Christ. Through His birth, death, and resurrection, we are citizens of His invisible kingdom on earth if we believe on Him and have accepted Him as Savior and Ruler of our hearts and lives. No, we haven't experienced the perfect righteousness throughout the earth promised in these verses; God's standards of righteous living and judgment have not become universal standards for humanity. But as we closely follow Christ, He becomes our *shelter from the wind* and *refuge from the storm*, the living stream of *water in the desert* and *the shadow of a great rock in a thirsty land* (verse 2). Praise His name!

5. The Lord has promised those who trust in Him that He is their shelter and refuge from the harsh winds and storms of life. When our path takes us through the hot and burning desert times, He provides life-giving refreshment and cooling, protective shade (Isaiah 49:10). Scripture records the testimonies of many that affirm the truth of these promises. From the following verses, list what the Lord is to His children.

   2 Samuel 22:2-3

   Psalm 9:9

   Psalm 62:6-7

   Isaiah 25:4

6. Record these verses:

   Isaiah 41:18

   Isaiah 49:10

7. Isaiah 32:2 speaks of the cool protection of a *shadow of a great rock*. Just as a large rock in the hot desert can

provide welcome shade for the weary traveler, when we go through the dry and discouraging times of life, if we trust God, we can rest quietly in the protection of the Rock of Ages. Record Isaiah 26:4.

8. According to the following verses, what does Jesus tell us He will provide for the thirsty?
   John 4:13-14

   Revelation 21:6

   Revelation 22:17

   Explain what you think this means.

Isaiah now inserts a warning to the women of Jerusalem who were living in luxury and ease and had become complacent and insensitive to their danger. This is a continuation of the warnings found in chapters 30 and 31. Isaiah contrasts their present lives of abundance and pleasure with the desolation and hardship that will soon destroy their security and their land. Instead of harboring this careless attitude and lack of concern, they should be trembling with fear and mourning in sorrow.

Isaiah then returns to the prophecy of future blessing. An outpouring of the Holy Spirit (see Joel 2:28-32) will not only restore the land but usher in a time of unparalleled fertility. A great outpouring of God's Holy Spirit took place at Pentecost (Acts 2:1-12). Complete fulfillment of the prophecy will take place in the messianic kingdom of the future. *GOD will be king over all the earth, one GOD and only one. What a Day that will be!* (Zechariah 14:9, TM)

9. What is the fruit (work) of righteousness?

   What is the effect (service) of righteousness? See Isaiah 32:17 (refer to the NIV or NASB).

Justice, righteousness, peace, security, and confidence are benefits from the presence of the Holy Spirit, not only in the kingdom of righteousness but also in my life and your life today.

# Reaping What They Sowed

**Read Isaiah 33:1-14.**

1. What will happen to the Assyrians *(destroyer)* when they are finished destroying and betraying?

2. In their prayer, Isaiah and the righteous remnant ask the Lord to be their _____ every morning and their _____ in time of distress.

3. Do you rely on God to be your strength? Record the following verses:

   Exodus 15:2

   2 Samuel 22:33

   Psalm 28:7

   Isaiah 40:29

Once again, Isaiah changes the mood from *behold* to *woe*. Punishment is followed by promise, promise by judgment. A final woe is pronounced against the Assyrian invaders under King Sennacherib and also against those who attempt to destroy God's people and their land in the latter days. *Do not be deceived: God cannot be mocked. A man reaps what he sows* (Galatians 6:7). God will repay! These treacherous destroyers will reap what they have sown. Judgment fits the sin.

Isaiah then intercedes for his people in prayer for the strength and salvation requested by King Hezekiah (2 Kings 19:3-4). Foolishly, Hezekiah and his advisers had trusted in a peace treaty with Sennacherib and their payment of tribute to him to save them (2 Kings 18:13-16). Now they confess that their efforts have proven futile; only trust in God can provide their salvation. Have you placed your total trust in Almighty God, or are you still trying to solve your problems through human efforts?

4. Praise follows promise; God is exalted! *He will fill Zion with _____ and _____. He*

*will be the sure foundation [stability] for your times, a rich store [wealth] of _____ and _____ and _____; the _____ ____ _____ _____ is the key to this treasure* (Isaiah 33:5-6).

5. After Isaiah affirms the sovereignty of God and the benefits of trusting Him, he pictures the deplorable situation in Judah. Describe in a word or two what has happened to:
   the brave men
   the envoys of peace
   the highways
   the peace treaty
   the people
   the land

Isaiah knew that all the people needed was God Almighty. "Man's extremity is God's opportunity," states Ross E. Price.[1] God had promised judgment against the Assyrians, and now He says He will act.

6. The Lord tells the Assyrians that their own methods will backfire on them. What will happen to the people?

Only God could have worked the miracle that defeated the mighty Assyrian army (Isaiah 37:36-37). And He waited until King Hezekiah and his people would know without a doubt that they were helpless to save themselves. God's methods and His timing are always wise and perfect.

God speaks to every nation and every age to learn from His judgment against Assyria. The godless will reap the harvest of their wickedness. This was true for the Assyrians, and it was true for the sinners in Zion. It is true for the godless today, and it will be true in the latter times when the Antichrist will arise and oppose everyone and everything that represents godliness and righteousness (2 Thessalonians 2:4). He, too, will be defeated in God's perfect timing (Revelation 19:20; 20:10).

God teaches us that it is not possible to save ourselves through our own strength. He sometimes allows weakness and defeat to make us strong and has promised, as Paul wrote, *"My grace is sufficient for you, for my power is made perfect in weakness." . . . That is why, for Christ's sake, I delight in weaknesses, in insults, in hardships, in persecutions, in difficulties. For when I am weak, then I am strong* (2 Corinthians 12:9-10).

Choose a verse from Day One that refers to God as a refuge, and record it.

# Reward for the Righteous

**Read Isaiah 33:14-24.**

1. Describe the reactions of the sinners and the godless.

2. Who or what is the consuming fire? Refer to Hebrews 12:29.

3. *Who of us can dwell with the consuming fire?* (Isaiah 33:14)

> There is a big difference between the flame of a candle and the roaring blast of a forest fire. We cannot even stand near a raging fire. Even with sophisticated firefighting equipment, a consuming fire is often beyond human control. God is not within our control either. We cannot force Him to do anything for us through our prayers. He cannot be contained. Yet, He is a God of compassion. He has saved us from sin, and He will save us from death. But everything that is worthless and sinful will be consumed by the fire of His wrath. Only what is good, dedicated to God, and righteous will remain.[1]

If we are to survive the fire of God's wrath, we must walk in godly righteousness, shunning every form of sin and evil. The reward for the righteous will be to *dwell on the heights* (verse 16) in God's protective and sustaining care.

4. Summarize Psalm 24:3-4.

Explain what you think is meant by *clean hands and a pure heart* (verse 4).

God requires a pure heart for us to have fellowship with Him (Matthew 5:8). Paul instructed young Timothy, *Keep yourself pure* (1 Timothy 5:22). David prayed for forgiveness, asking God to cleanse and make him clean (Psalm 51:7) and to *create in me a pure heart . . . and renew a steadfast spirit within me* (Psalm 51:10).

5. Summarize or record these verses:

   2 Timothy 2:22

   1 John 1:7-9

The blood of Christ makes us clean, but "to be pure means to keep ourselves morally straight, free from the corruption of sin. God also purifies us, but there is action we must take to remain morally fit."[2]

The frightened people of Jerusalem were mourning for the loss of city after city and for the devastated land. Isaiah assures them that they will once again see a peaceful Jerusalem; they will no longer see the arrogant Assyrian army encamped about them.

Someday we will see a New Jerusalem, a permanent dwelling place of peace and beauty where our Lord and Savior will reign in perfect righteousness. Sin and evil will have been totally eliminated, consumed by divine fire, and "our God [will be] a River of grace . . . where no enemy galley can come." *The LORD will be king over the whole earth. On that day there will be one LORD, and his name the only name. . . . Jerusalem will be raised up and remain in its place. . . . It will be inhabited; never again will it be destroyed. Jerusalem will be secure* (Zechariah 14:9-11).

6. Read Revelation 21:1—22:5, and list several of the blessings we will enjoy in the Holy City, the New Jerusalem.

"In the promise to Jerusalem, [Isaiah 33:] 17-22, Dr. [Phineas F.] Bresee saw 'The Defense of the Sanctified.' (1) God's righteousness surrounds every life that is fully surrendered to Him; (2) The glorious Lord gives His people pleasant places and ample protection, 21; (3) The Lord . . . will save us, and His saving work is an uttermost salvation."[3]

*I know what I'm doing. I have it all planned out—plans to take care of you, not abandon you, plans to give you the future you hope for* (Jeremiah 29:11, TM).

Be prepared to share a specific way in which the Lord has been good to you and blessed you because you took refuge (trusted) in Him.

## DAYS FOUR AND FIVE

# Righteous Retribution

**Read Isaiah 34.**

*Isaiah 34 presents a picture of a God of anger, wrath, judgment, and destruction. It has become fashionable, politically correct, among some theologians and their followers to deny this aspect of God's holy character and to declare that a God of love could not act in vengeance against a nation nor condemn an individual to hell. That is a clear denial of the truth of Scripture. Others have taken the opposite view and refuse to submit to a God they see only as vengeful and angry. That is a denial of the mercy, love, and compassion that compelled God to give His only Son to the sinful world as a sacrifice for our sins so that in believing on Him we might have restoration and relationship with God.*

*DAY FOUR is a study of the result of God's anger against all who have opposed Him and His people, as recorded in Isaiah 34. DAY FIVE is a study of the reason for God's anger, and His plea for repentance.*

### DAY FOUR
#### THE RESULT OF GOD'S JUDGMENT ON THE NATIONS

1. Look up "retribution" in a dictionary, and record the definition.

2. With whom is the Lord angry?

   What will happen to the nations and their armies?

   What will occur in nature?

Isaiah 34 addresses the final conflict with Satan and his forces and the wrath of God that will be poured out in judgment. In Isaiah 1:2, God called on heaven and earth (also see Psalm 50:3-4, 6) to witness His judgment on His people, the nation of Israel. In Isaiah 34:1, God calls on the nations of the earth and their people to witness His final judgment upon all nations. This will be a slaughter and destruction the world has never experienced. Total destruction of enemy armies had been predicted before, but God's fury will now

destroy so completely that there will be too many killed even to permit proper burial. Judgment will be universal, and it will be severe.

3. Summarize the following verses:

   Isaiah 13:9-13 (Matthew 24:29)

   Isaiah 66:15-16

   2 Peter 3:10

4. Compare Isaiah 34:4 with Revelation 6:12-14. What similarities do you find?

The nation of Edom is singled out as receiving God's judgment (see Ezekiel 25:14). Edom has been in conflict after conflict with Israel. The two nations share a common ancestry: Israel is descended from Jacob, Edom from his twin brother, Esau (Genesis 25:19-26). Edom is a symbolic figure for all those who are rebellious toward God, His land, and His people. (Note: In Genesis 12:3 God promises to bless those who bless His people and curse those who curse His people.) The wild beasts symbolize the leaders of the rebellious nations and possibly the rulers of Satan's forces of darkness as well.

5. What will become of the following in Edom? (Isaiah 34:9, 13)

   Streams
   Dust
   Land
   Citadels
   Strongholds

   What will possess the land? (verses 11, 13-15)

The land of Edom will be completely barren and desolate, overgrown with nettles, thorns, and brambles and inhabited only by wild beasts and birds of prey. The words translated *chaos* and *desolation* in verse 11 are the same Hebrew words translated *without form, and void* in Genesis 1:2 (KJV). The land will burn with unquenchable fire; its smoke will rise forever. The Edomites had once refused to allow the Israelites to pass through their land (Numbers 20:14-21); now no one will ever pass through the land again. Vengeance on God's enemies will mean validation for God's people.[1] There will be no escape. This is a picture of conditions in the heavens and on earth at the time of the final conflict (Revelation 16 and 18).

6.  God had commanded Isaiah to write down the prophecies God had revealed to him. Why? Refer to Isaiah 30:8.


This *scroll of the Lord* (34:16) we are to look in and read probably refers to Isaiah's writings of inspired prophecy. Anyone living at the time of God's judgment of Edom will be able to read the prophecies and affirm the truth of God's Word. "Scripture is God's witness to His own faithfulness."[2]

## MEMORY CHALLENGE

What should we taste and see?

Who is blessed?

## DAY FIVE
### The Reason for God's Wrath and the Plea for Repenteance

Based on the writings of Josh McDowell and Don Stewart, *Answers to Tough Questions*, and *The Oxford Companion to the Bible*, edited by Bruce M. Metzger and Michael D. Coogan.

1.  Summarize these verses:

    Jeremiah 10:10



    Hebrews 10:30-31




"One of the frequent accusations against the Bible is that it contains two different conceptions of God. The Old Testament allegedly presents only a God of wrath, while the New Testament allegedly depicts only a God of love."[1] However, a careful study of Scripture reveals that this is not the case. God is presented over and over in the Old Testament as a God of mercy and love.

"The Lord is a merciful God, but He is also a holy God; His 'vengeance is an expression of his holiness.' He cannot let sin go unpunished. His vengeance is essentially a response to evil. [It is] punishment in retribution for injury . . . and the word seldom has a connotation of vindictiveness . . . God's vengeance is balanced by his mercy (Ps. 103:10). Vengeance, then, is very much a part of God's character and does not contradict His love."[2]

"God would not have destroyed . . . nations except that He is a God of justice and that their evil could not go unchecked and condoned. He did intend and desire to punish them as

a part of His plan, in consistency with His holy nature and jealousy for His . . . people" if these nations refuse to repent of their evil ways.[3]

God is patient. He gave them repeated opportunities to repent; He gives us repeated opportunities to repent. It is only when we continually refuse that God punishes us in judgment for our evil deeds.

2.  Record or summarize these verses:

    Job 34:10-12


    Proverbs 29:1


    Ezekiel 18:23


    Romans 2:5-6, 8


    Colossians 3:25


*God is love* (1 John 4:8) and love and mercy, as well as judgment, are shown throughout the Old Testament, and judgment, as well as love, is found throughout the New Testament. "God is consistent and unchanging, but different situations call for different emphases. Therefore, when the two testaments are read the way they were intended, they reveal the same holy God who is rich in mercy, but who will not let sin go unpunished."[4]

3.  Summarize Romans 1:18-20.




"Since wrongs are not always righted in the present and God's vengeance is delayed because of his patience [we] look forward to a 'day of vengeance' in the future . . . that will mark the beginning of a new age."[5]

4.  Have you responded to God's love and compassion by accepting His gift of mercy and grace and forgiveness for sin? Record or summarize these verses:

    John 3:16



    Romans 5:8



    Romans 10:13

Ephesians 1:7-8

Ephesians 2:4-5

2 Peter 3:9b

1 John 3:1a

If you have asked God to forgive your sins and you are living in obedience to Him, you need not fear the Day of Judgment; your name is recorded in the Book of Life (Revelation 3:5; 20:12; 21:27). *At that time [His] people—everyone whose name is found written in the book—will be delivered* (Daniel 12:1). Instead of going into eternal doom, you will enter into eternal life in the presence and glory of the Lord (Romans 2:7; 1 John 2:17). *For the wages of sin is death, but the gift of God is eternal life in Christ Jesus our Lord* (Romans 6:23).

*All my inmost being, praise his holy name* (Psalm 103:1).

> The love of God is greater far
>     Than tongue or pen can ever tell;
> It goes beyond the highest star,
>     And reaches to the lowest hell.
> The guilty pair, bowed down with care,
>     God gave His Son to win;
> His erring child He reconciled,
>     And pardoned from his sin.
>
> O love of God, how rich and pure!
>     How measureless and strong!
> It shall forevermore endure—
>     The saints' and angels' song!
>
> —Frederick M. Lehman

## MEMORY CHALLENGE

Fill in the blanks:

_____ *and* _____ *that the* _____ _____ \_\_\_\_\_;
_____ *is the man who* _____ _____ *in him.*

Psalm 34:8

## DAY SIX

# Restoration and Rejoicing

**Read Isaiah 35.**

1. Contrast the condition of the land in Isaiah 34:9-11 with 35:1-2.

    Record Romans 8:21.

2. What does God tell Isaiah to *say to those with fearful hearts* (verse 4)?

3. Explain the transformation in the following:

    The feeble hands and knees
    The blind eyes
    The deaf ears
    The lame
    The mute tongue

4. Compare verses 6b- 7 with Isaiah 34:9, 11-13.

In chapters 1—34, Isaiah has delivered a message of judgment interspersed with promises of hope for the remnant of faithful believers. Chapter 35 pictures the kingdom of righteousness that God will establish after the destruction of evil at the Day of Judgment. The fires of judgment now will have burned out; God will have sheathed His sword of destruction. The curse of sin will have been removed.

The land will be totally transformed. Water will gush forth in the dry and arid desert, which will *burst into bloom . . . and shout for joy* (verse 2). The blossoming desert also symbolizes the change in the life of the believer. No longer is the believer's heart dry and arid and filled with sin; now it is a heart filled with joy and the reflection of the love of Jesus Christ. "The change of the environment from a desert to a garden might have been miraculous, but it is nothing compared to the transformation of the human spirit."[1]

Feeble hands, symbols of powerlessness, will be strength-ened; weak knees will be strong and steady to take us in the right direction. The strength of God will replace our weakness. Praise the Lord! No longer will God's people need to live with fearful hearts, in constant dread of attack and destruction. God will have intervened to rescue His people and establish righteousness. Blind eyes will see, and deaf ears will hear, both physically and spiritually. All humanity will be able to see and hear and discern the truth. The ministry of Jesus began the fulfillment of this promise. Complete fulfillment will take place in His glori-ous reign of righteousness when He returns in power and glory after the Judgment.

5.  What will God provide for His returning remnant?


What will it be called?


What will not be found there? (verses 8-9)


*Only the _____ will walk there, and the*

*_____ of the LORD will return* (verses 9-10).


Some of the most joyous occasions in Israel's history had been the annual feasts when pilgrims would journey to Jerusalem, singing and praising God along the way. A few roads had been built in Israel for these pilgrimages, mostly narrow, rocky, winding, and dangerous footpaths. The ma-jor roads for merchant caravans bypassed the mountainous terrain around Jerusalem. Roads were not built across stretches of desert and shifting sands during ancient times. But this land will no longer be a desert, and a wonderful highway will be provided for the return of the ransomed and redeemed to the beautiful city of Zion (Revelation 21:18-27). No unclean person will walk on this highway, nor will the foolish sinner. This is God's highway for His faith-ful remnant, where travelers will be completely protected and perfectly secure.

6.  Why do you think this highway will be called *the Way of Holiness* (verse 8)? What is the way of holiness?



Record phrases from the following verses, and use them to help you with your answers.

    Deuteronomy 18:13



    Deuteronomy 28:9

Romans 12:1-2


2 Corinthians 7:1


Ephesians 1:4a


1 Thessalonians 4:7


1 Peter 1:14-16


"The Highway of Holiness is the theme of this chapter [Isa-iah 35]. Pilgrims enter the way through the tollgate called dedication. (1) They pursue the way with a dependable source of direction, 8c; (2) They have assurance of protec-tion from contamination by the unclean, 8b, and from rav-enous beasts, 9; (3) Travelers on the holy way are com-pelled by a conviction of mission, 1, 5-7; (4) They shall reach their destination triumphantly, 10."[2] To walk in the way of holiness is to be set apart for God, obedient to His will and commands, staying morally and spiritually pure.

The promise in Isaiah 35:10 is so glorious that Isaiah re-peats it word for word in 51:11. Homecoming for the be-liever will be a time of unparalleled joy and gladness. No more sorrow! No more sighing!

> *There'll be singing, there'll be shouting*
> *when the saints come marching home,*
> *In Jerusalem, in Jerusalem;*
> *Waving palms with loud hosannas*
> *as the King shall take His throne,*
> *In the new Jerusalem.*
> —C. B. Widmeyer

Hallelujah! Praise the Lord!

*Written by Helen Silvey*

## MEMORY CHALLENGE

Write Psalm 34:8 from memory.

# Isaiah

**LESSON 9**

■ A Study of Isaiah, Chapters 36—37

---

*The next two lessons of Isaiah are on Isaiah 36—39, which is a historical interlude between the first and second halves of the book. Chronologically, Isaiah 38—39 come before chapters 36 and 37. Isaiah 36—37 are retrospective, while chapters 38—39 are prospective.*

## DAY ONE

# Intimidation

**Read Isaiah 36:1-10.**
(Optional reading: 2 Kings 18:17-25)

1. Explain Jerusalem's situation as described in Isaiah 36:1-2*a*.

2. On the map note all the cities of Judah. Circle the one from which the king of Assyria sent his field commander.

3. The field commander's intimidation is fourfold. List the points:

   (1) verse 5—

   (2) verse 6—

   (3) verse 7—

   (4) verse 10—

4. Do you see intimidation here? Look up "intimidation" in a dictionary, and give its definition.

5. Describe a situation in which you remember feeling intimidated.

6. How did you handle the intimidation? What was your strategy? Did it overwhelm you?

---

## MEMORY CHALLENGE

# Psalm 34:9

*Fear the LORD, you his saints,
for those who fear him lack nothing.*

7. Israel had been taught that its main strategy for intimidation was confidence in God. But the field commander asked, *On what are you basing this confidence of yours?* (verse 4). Then he mocked the fact that they might say, *We are depending on the LORD our God* (verse 7). The Israelites needed to remember their history of God's care. Summarize the following scriptures.

Exodus 14:9-10, 21-31

1 Samuel 17:8-11, 45-50

2 Chronicles 20:1-4, 15, 22

8. Record these promises from Psalms that the Israelites could have claimed.

Psalm 3:3*a*

Psalm 18:29*a*

Psalm 20:7

Psalm 91:4

9. Summarize these promises regarding confidence in the Lord.

Psalm 27:1

Psalm 118:6-7

Jeremiah 17:7-8

10. Jumping ahead in the story, summarize what Hezekiah told the people to do in this situation as found in 2 Chronicles 32:7-8. Specifically point out what the people gained.

As Isaiah 36 opens, we see Sennacherib, the king of Assyria, marching on Jerusalem. He had already taken 46 fortified cities of Judah. If I lived in number 47, I would be worried!

Sennacherib used his Rabshakeh, a military title for field commander, to make the conquest easier. He sent him ahead to intimidate the people. If he could frighten them and undermine their morale, maybe they would surrender. It was one thing to say Judah had no military strength and another to say Egypt could not help them. But the field commander went too far when he said God would be no help. Now he was challenging the validity of the God of Judah.

Furthermore, the Rabshakeh called the Judean king by his name, Hezekiah—but he referred to his own king, Sennacherib, as the king of Assyria. This added to his intimidation efforts, implying that these two kings were not on the same level. If we read ahead in the story to tomorrow's scripture, we will also see that the field commander shouted his negations within earshot of the soldiers, who would tell everyone in town. Hezekiah's representatives wanted privacy. It was intimidating to have the common folk know all the business of the king and the government.

So the scene is set. What Sennacherib and Assyria did not know was that Judah had a secret weapon. Isaiah was the representative of the secret weapon, and he had already prophesied about this time. In Isaiah 8:4-10 he stated that the northern kingdom of Israel would be overrun by the Assyrians. But the king of Assyria, who would be confident in his own strength, would find out that God was really in charge. Isaiah advised, *Devise your strategy, but it will be thwarted; propose your plan, but it will not stand, for God is with us* (verse 10). Isaiah's heart was firm with the Psalmist that *I will not fear the tens of thousands drawn up against me on every side* (3:6). Judah's secret weapon was the Almighty God!

In human affairs intimidation can be a powerful strategy. I remember a time when as a 24-year-old social worker, I visited a client who lived in a dangerous apartment complex. She was bright and had tremendous potential, and I was attempting to get her into college. But she had recently been released from prison and was quite a rough character. She was intimidating herself, but her brother was even more so. He got in my face, pushed me, and asked some pointed questions. I knew he was trying to intimidate me, and it was working—because I was scared! But I remember thinking how important it was not to show my fear. He didn't need to know that what I was saying over and over in my mind and heart was *God, help me! God, help me!* Shortly after this, my agency could not visit these apartments without a police escort, but that day my only confidence was in the Lord!

I might have melted like wax from fear that day had I not believed that God was my Protector. My only confidence was in Him. I had no other resource. Neither did Jerusalem when the king of Assyria was moving to their town. They had no military strength, no tribute, and no powerful foreign alliance. Now they were where God could get their attention. Stand back to see how He delivered them in the exciting conclusion of the story!

# Insinuations

**Read Isaiah 36:11-22.**
(Optional reading: 2 Kings 18:26-37)

1. What was the request of Eliakim, Shebna, and Joah? Why was it turned down?

2. Webster defines insinuation as an "indirect or sly hint" or "as gently gaining favor." The Assyrian field commander was trying to insinuate that Jerusalem had their trust misplaced. Who were the two he said would not deliver them?

3. In yesterday's lesson you listed the fourfold intimidations of the field commander. These could also be reasons to surrender without a fight. Continue the list according to the following verses.

   (1) Isaiah 36:14-15, 18

   (2) 36:16-17

   (3) 36:18-20

4. What was the response of the people to the field commander's insinuations?

5. Summarize these examples of insinuation from the following scriptures.

   Genesis 39:6b-7, 11-15

   Nehemiah 4:1-3

6. Insinuation is a form of indirect communication, as opposed to being straightforward. List some dangers of indirect communication.

7. Record the following scriptures regarding our straightforward communication.

   Proverbs 10:32

   Matthew 5:37

   1 Corinthians 1:5

   2 Timothy 2:16

Some may say that the field commander would never fit in our day because he was being "politically incorrect." He was trying to arouse the residents of Jerusalem against their king and God instead of going through the proper channels of addressing the counselors to the king. When asked to be appropriate by speaking Aramaic, the language for international discourse, he became even more snide.

His tactic was to convince them to yield to Assyria and better their condition, even though they would have to abandon their God. He made it sound as if the people would get liberty, when in truth they would get slavery. Although he was bold in his statements, the underlying insinuation was that Jerusalem could never win.

Let's look at this issue of insinuation. What's wrong with it? An insinuation is unclear; the message is vague. This is a form of manipulation that leads to misunderstandings and is often hurtful.

Direct and honest communication leaves no doubt, confusion, misunderstanding, or hurt. What is meant is clear. The purpose is not to manipulate or get one's own way.

As we talk with each other, we better represent Christ when we are straightforward with our meaning. We do not want to deceive in any way. Our culture has learned to avoid direct communication because we don't want to hurt anyone's feelings—or we just aren't willing to face tough issues. Many people hate confrontations, so they deal with it in subtle ways instead of directly. In the long run, this is far more hurtful, because it closes channels to solve problems. Resentments and hurt feelings can last for years.

Several months ago a friend hurt me deeply. I am confident it was not purposeful, but it was a result of her indirect communication. As I was trying to decide how to deal with it, my first instinct was to go to another friend, tell her what happened, and get sympathy. The Lord said, "No, Linda. You would be doing the very thing she did to you that was hurtful. If it's important enough to discuss, discuss it with the person who hurt you. If not, keep your mouth shut." I don't think I'm alone in being tempted to indirect communication. It's a trap and a form of deceit. But Jesus says, *Simply let your "Yes" be "Yes," and your "No," "No"* (Matthew 5:37). This obviously points out that we should be honest and direct.

Indirect communication can become a habit. But, praise God, we can ask His Holy Spirit to help us conquer this habit. Then we can make a choice to communicate directly. The more we do so, the more comfortable we get with it, and it becomes a part of our being that better represents Christ.

## MEMORY CHALLENGE

Write out this week's memory verse several times below.

## DAY THREE

# Intervention

**Read Isaiah 37:1-15.**
(Optional reading: 2 Kings 19:1-7)

1. Today's scripture contains the third recorded response to the field commander's intimidations. Remember that the people on the wall were silent. How did Eliakim, Shebna, and Joah respond at the end of Isaiah 36? Then how did Hezekiah respond?

2. What did the three administrators of Hezekiah tell Isaiah, and what was his answer?

3. We could summarize Isaiah's answer with this week's memory challenge. Write it here.

4. Hezekiah took two actions to intervene in this crisis. What were they?

5. Hezekiah's interventions showed that his confidence and hope were in God. Sennacherib had destroyed every nation, city, and god he had gone up against, yet Hezekiah believed Jerusalem could be different. Summarize the verses that support his view:

Exodus 20:2-6

2 Samuel 7:22

Psalm 86:8

Jeremiah 35:15

6. Hezekiah's thoughts at this point had to be something like those of Psalm 143. Summarize it below.

All through the scriptures of Days 1-3, the Assyrians have intimidated and insinuated that the God of Israel is just like any other god. This was based on the belief of the day that each nation or people had a god. If that nation was powerful, their god was powerful. It would seem that Assyria's god, Asshur, was very powerful for Sennacherib's unbroken list of conquests was proof.

The field commander was claiming that God had ordained that the Assyrians were to rule everyone, so why fight? He thought Jerusalem had given up on God because they had taken down His altars on the high places. We know that those altars were for worshiping false gods, and Hezekiah had cleaned up that evil. His actions showed greater commitment and service to God, not loss of confidence.

Hezekiah was not frightened away from following the Lord. He was frightened before the Lord. Isaiah assured him that the Rabshakeh had "blasphemed" Yahweh by his misbeliefs about the power of gods and by misrepresenting the circumstances of the altars to false gods. Isaiah further predicted that the Lord would put a spirit in the king of Assyria *so that when he hears a certain report [concerning Egypt's attack], he will return to his own country* (Isaiah 37:7).

When Hezekiah needed an intervention, he went to the Lord. He sent his administrators to a prophet he could trust, and he himself went to the Temple. Tomorrow we will see that in the Temple he turned a day of trouble into a day of prayer.

When we need an intervention, do we go to the Lord? There are many choices. Which do you pick? Meditate on this thought, and ask the Holy Spirit to affirm or convict you.

## MEMORY CHALLENGE

Find another verse regarding fearing the Lord, and record it. Look in Psalms or Proverbs or a Bible concordance for this.

## DAY FOUR

# Intercession

**Read Isaiah 37:14-20.**
(Optional reading: 2 Kings 19:1-13)

1. Give examples of the following from Hezekiah's prayer.

   Praise:

   Problem:

   Petition:

2. Hezekiah had actually tried a different tactic before going to the Temple to pray. Summarize what he did, as described in 2 Kings 18:13-16.

3. Hezekiah, however, was a godly king. Summarize what you learn from 2 Chronicles 29:1-2.

4. Intercession can be defined as "prayer offered in behalf of others" *(Guideposts Family Concordance)*. Give examples of the pattern Hezekiah used of praise, problem, and petition in each of the following prayers used by other godly men. Then find the element missing from Hezekiah's prayer that is in all three of these.

   Jehoshaphat in 2 Chronicles 20:6-12

   Ezra in Ezra 9:6-15

   Nehemiah in Nehemiah 1:5-11

5. These godly men made intercession for their people. Who makes intercession for us? Read the following passages.

   John 17:9, 20
   Romans 8:26-27, 34
   Hebrews 7:24-25

6. We in turn make intercession for each other. Record phrases from Ephesians 1:15-18.

In 701 B.C. Sennacherib invaded and laid siege to Jerusalem. Hezekiah averted that problem by giving him the gold and silver from the Temple and palace. Now Sennacherib was back. This time Hezekiah sent his advisers to Isaiah, and he went into the Temple to pray. Hezekiah was known for his faith and his prayer. He humbled himself before the Lord for an answer in time of crisis. He turned a day of trouble into a day of prayer.

Jeannie McCullough, founder and teacher of Wisdom of the Word, reflected in the Introduction to Isaiah that Hezekiah's prayer had four r's. First, he *removed* himself from distractions so he could pray by going to the Temple. Second, he *responded* to the Lord in prayer. Third, he *reminded* God that he had walked with Him, that he had been faithful in truth and that he had been loyal. Hezekiah pointed out that his loyalty included a heart that was God's. Finally, the king *released* his burden.

The pattern we have looked at in prayer today included praise, pointing out the problem, and petition. As Hezekiah presented his problem to God, he pointed out heavenly truths and earthly facts. It was so simple! This pattern often includes confession, as we see in the prayers of Jehoshaphat, Ezra, and Nehemiah.

So intercession was Hezekiah's plan. He was praying to God on behalf of his people. We have also been given this wonderful opportunity of praying for each other. It is a privilege and a gift to bring someone else to the Father for safety, salvation, conviction, wisdom, and guidance. We are intercessors.

But the best has been saved for last: *Christ* is constantly interceding for *us!* Intercession is His eternal work! Hezekiah was limited to time, space, desire, and discipline, just as we are. But Christ is not. He is constantly taking our prayers and pleading with the Father on our behalf. When we are negligent to pray or unable or just don't know how, He is interceding for us. Don't you want to praise Him and thank Him for that right now?

## MEMORY CHALLENGE

Did Hezekiah fear the Lord or Sennacherib more? Quote today's memory verse aloud.

## DAY FIVE

# Insolence

**Read Isaiah 37:21-29.**
(Optional reading: 2 Kings 19:20-28)

1. Webster defines insolence as "contemptuous or overbearing language or manner; insulting behavior; offensive impertinence." How does the Lord describe Sennacherib's insolence in Isaiah 37:21-25?

2. The king of Assyria believed he had caused all the fortified cities of Israel to become piles of stone. What was the truth?

3. Why does God plan to put a hook in the nose of Sennacherib?

4. Summarize Numbers 15:30-31, which further tells the fate of the insolent.

5. The opposite of being contemptuous or insulting to the Lord would be to bless Him and lift His Name on high. Summarize the following scriptures.

Nehemiah 9:5b-6

Psalm 63:4

Psalm 96:4, 7

Psalm 145:1-3

6. Record your own favorite scripture about blessing or praising the Lord. If you need help in finding a verse, look up "praise" in a Bible concordance, or read a chapter from Psalms.

"In this time of the nation's supreme peril Isaiah stepped forth in his greatness as a man of God. Knowing that the very national existence of Judah would shortly be at stake, he no longer sought to alarm and dishearten the people. His words became vibrant with encouragement and hope."[1] Isaiah reminded them that the king of Assyria could not blaspheme the name of God without retribution. All of Sennacherib's success was because God allowed it. But now he would be made to return the way he came. Jerusalem would be saved.

In Luke 12:16-20 Jesus told a similar story about a rich fool who thought his success was due to his own hand—so he decided to build bigger storage barns in order to be able to take it easy the rest of his life. *But God said to him, "You fool! This very night your life will be demanded from you"* (verse 20). God determined the life of that man, as He does everyone.

Madalyn Murray O'Hair became a household name in the United States during the 1960s. She hated anything to do with God and was on a mission to remove His name from all government workings. She fought organized prayer in schools, the motto "In God we trust" on coins, and "under God" in the Pledge of Allegiance to the flag. She felt these infringed upon her rights as an atheist. She mocked the name of God, insulting Him.

In 1946 when she was pregnant with her first child, Ms. O'Hair announced to her family during a thunderstorm, "I'm going out in that storm to challenge God to strike me and this child dead with one of those lightning bolts. Come and watch!" When the audience was in place, "She shook her hand menacingly toward the heavens and, at the top of her voice, unleashed blasphemies intended to provoke violent wrath from God." When that did not happen, she strode triumphantly inside the house proclaiming she had just proved that God did not exist. "If God exists, he would surely have taken up my challenge."[2]

For a season she had success, at least as far as being well known and accomplishing some of her goals. She was spreading propaganda to the public and financially became stable through donations to her cause.

But God was not going to let an insolent woman succeed forever. "She had demanded things of God. And when He had refused her demands, she had fought with Him openly."[3] Who was she to challenge God? The biggest blow to her was when her son, William J. Murray, became a Christian.

What Bill experienced growing up in his mother's home was anger, neglect, bitterness, manipulation, and lack of love. His adult life became a nightmare as he had difficulty with jobs, alcohol, and relationships. Somehow the way of life he had been taught did not add up to him, and he began to believe there was something better.

In his search for God, Bill Murray had a dream one night. It began as a terrible graphic nightmare that ended with a huge sword pointed at a Bible with Latin words that meant "by this symbol conquer."[4] He arose and went to a 24-hour store to buy a Bible. The Gospel of Luke taught him of a personal Savior, Jesus Christ, whom he invited into his heart right then. Bill Murray made a U-turn, apologizing along the way to many, including the city of Baltimore for his part in removing Bible reading and public prayer from the schools. He now works to serve Christ with his life.

Madalyn Murray O'Hair was missing for over 10 years before she was proclaimed dead.

Whether in 688 B.C. or today, God will not allow contempt of Him forever. One of His attributes is judgment. Whether the judgment comes in this lifetime or after death, it will come. But isn't it joyous that we may bless the Lord instead of insult Him—and in return receive His blessings for obedience? Then He truly is our Defender and Protector and Deliverer. Bless the Lord!

## MEMORY CHALLENGE

What will we lack if we fear the Lord?

# Incredible!

**Read Isaiah 37:30-38.**
(Optional reading: 2 Kings 19:29-37)

1. What Isaiah prophesied regarding the king of Assyria was incredible. Summarize Isaiah 37:33-35.

2. What were the signs the Lord gave to Hezekiah in verses 30-32?

3. What was the incredible deliverance of the Lord (verses 33-36)?

4. Would you not agree that this was a miracle? Summarize four other miracles.

   **Old Testament**

   1 Kings 17:7-9, 12-16

   1 Kings 18:21-39

   **New Testament**

   Matthew 14:15-21

   Luke 8:22-25

5. Describe a favorite miracle from the Old Testament and one from the New Testament. If you are new to the study of God's Word, listen to the stories from your group, or turn to the Gospel of Matthew for a miracle.

6. Do you have a personal story of the incredible workings of God in your life? Make a note of the story below, and if you're comfortable doing so, share it with your group, for it will be a great source of encouragement.

Isaiah prophesied that in 12 months the land would be clear of invaders, and agriculture would resume its course. This was a great comfort and assurance to the people—like the promise of springtime.

Isaiah then made an incredible prophecy—he stated that the king of Assyria would not enter the city nor *come before it with shield* (verse 33). What a bold prophecy regarding a man who had overrun 46 fortified cities in a row! But this promise of protection was based on God's concern for His own honor and regard for His covenant with David.

But the story gets even more incredible. God sent an angel of the Lord, and in one night he put to death 185,000 Assyrian soldiers! Can you imagine being one of the guards on the wall in Jerusalem? The first sight you would see at sunrise would be a sea of corpses instead of the Assyrian camp full of soldiers milling around. Would it be called anything but a miracle? To say that Sennacherib *broke camp and withdrew* (verse 37) was an understatement. I'm sure he couldn't get out of there fast enough!

Verse 38 tells us that after returning home, about 16 years later, Sennacherib was assassinated by two of his sons. He met a tragic end as insolent people often do.

Isn't God incredible? At a time when Judah needed an incredible man, God sent Isaiah. Through many wicked kings, God sent an incredibly godly king, Hezekiah. The prophet gave an incredibly bold message. Finally, the deliverance by the angel of the Lord was incredible!

Don't you think that Isaiah and Hezekiah and all of Jerusalem knew God in a more incredible way after this event? Yes, if they so chose. A miraculous event in our lives moves us closer to God only if we allow it to increase our faith and belief. Not all of those who saw Christ's miracles in the New Testament allowed Him to change their hearts or lives. They still had to choose to do so.

Somewhere, at some time in your life, you have witnessed an incredible event. Maybe it was deliverance as with the Assyrian army, or maybe it was a changed life. Maybe it was someone unbelievably bold for the Lord, or maybe it was a healing. Did you let it expand your faith and belief in God? Go back to that moment in your mind now, and let it increase your confidence in God. He is incredible!

*Written by Linda Shaw*

## MEMORY CHALLENGE

Psalm 34:7 is so relevant to today's lesson. Quote aloud Psalm 34:7-9.

**Bible Study Series**

# Isaiah

## ■ A Study of Isaiah, Chapters 38—39

**LESSON 10**

---

## DAY ONE

# Terminal

Read Isaiah 38, concentrating on verse 1.

1. What was Hezekiah's message from Isaiah?

2. What would you do to *put your house in order* if you were told you would soon die?

3. What would you do differently on a daily basis, if anything, if you knew you had only a short time to live?

4. *Guideposts Family Concordance* defines the word "eternal" as "without end." How were the following situations representative of someone thinking more of the eternal (lasting moment) than the present moment?

   Nehemiah 2:1-5

   Esther 4:15-16

   John 19:38-40

   Acts 9:10-17

5. What do we know about the importance of the eternal?

   John 6:68

   John 10:28

   John 17:3

   Romans 6:23

   Titus 3:5-7

---

## MEMORY CHALLENGE

# Psalm 34:10

*The lions may grow weak and hungry, but those who seek the LORD lack no good thing.*

6. Personalize 2 Corinthians 4:16-18 as a reminder of what is lasting.

Hezekiah was told he was terminal. He was given a death sentence. This occurred the same year as the siege of Jerusalem. (Remember that Isaiah 38 and 39 chronologically came before Isaiah 36 and 37). The disappointment and stress were just too much, and Hezekiah turned his face to the wall and wept and prayed. He didn't want to die. He wasn't ready. He was in the prime of life, and he had great hopes for his kingdom. Also at this time Hezekiah had no son and therefore no heir to the throne.

Have you ever been pronounced terminal? If not, can you imagine how it might feel—to find out suddenly one day that the illness you suffer from you would not recover from? The shock, the fear, and the sadness would be overwhelming.

Betty Rollin, an NBC news correspondent, had a similar experience when in the prime of life and good health she found out she had breast cancer. Her story is told in her book *First You Cry*,[1] which 25 years later is now considered a classic. She wrote about her obsession with her illness and how what was important to her in life changed during that time. Fear of how it would all work out was often overwhelming, and many of her relationships became strained. It was difficult to work, and at times she could not quit crying. There was anger at the doctors for not diagnosing her sooner when she had been under their care. There was loss—a part of her body was missing. Life became a struggle as everything suddenly focused on whether or not she would live. Cancer made her entire life different. That difference did not feel good.

So it was with Hezekiah. It didn't feel good, and he, too, cried. But whereas Betty Rollin made some poor choices about how to handle her illness, Hezekiah prayed. The man of prayer handled "terminal" with prayer.

That does not mean that Hezekiah did not go through the stages of grief most of us do when facing a serious loss. He probably started out in denial—and then in verse two we see glimpses of the next three stages of grief. Turning his face to the wall probably indicates some depression regarding the pronouncement of "terminal." The fact that he "wept bitterly" might show some anger. Finally, the prayer itself was a bargaining with God to see if He would consider changing His diagnosis. Hezekiah asked for a sign of his healing and with that moved to the last stage of grief, which is acceptance. In his case acceptance was easy, for he was to be healed. It is much harder when the pronouncement is still "terminal."

Anyone is subject to being stricken with an illness. In *Matthew Henry's Commentary* he states, "Neither men's greatness nor their goodness will exempt them from the arrests of sickness and death. Hezekiah, a potentate on earth and a favorite of Heaven is struck with a disease, which, without a miracle, will certainly be mortal; and this in the midst of his days and usefulness."[2] Betty Rollin never believed it would happen to her, for she had always been in great health. She rarely even got a cold.

But maybe the point is what we do with it when such a pronouncement of "terminal" comes. Does it make us think of what is really important in life? What really matters? What about my life is truly eternal?

With so many responsibilities it is easy for our lives to get pressed by the urgent instead of the important. As I write this today on January 8, it seems rather urgent that I get my outdoor Christmas lights down. But is that really so important? What if they were up until January 20? Would that make any difference in eternity? No, but hopefully choosing to write this lesson today will. Only God knows that, but certainly Bible study is more important than Christmas lights.

How would you live your life differently if the time were short? Oklahoma experienced its third major tragedy in six years on January 27, 2001. Ten men connected with the Oklahoma State University (OSU) basketball program were killed in a tragic plane crash. Suddenly sports competition was not so important. "I told our team that life is so precious and sometimes we take it for granted," said Eddie Sutton, coach of the OSU Cowboys. "One thing they must understand is they better live every day like it might be the last. They certainly understand that (now)."[3]

What we do that is eternal—a loving hug, encouraging a friend, time spent in prayer, a lesson taught a child or memorizing God's Word—these are the things that will last and make a difference in someone's life. Don't wait to be pronounced "terminal" to make eternal moments important in your life.

*Father, help us to keep focused on what really matters and spend our time loving and serving You and others. In Jesus' name we pray. Amen.*

# Tears

**Read Isaiah 38:2-3.**
(Optional reading: 2 Kings 20:2-3)

1. What did Hezekiah pray to the Lord?


2. Summarize the following scriptures, which could represent Hezekiah's emotions.

   Psalm 6:6


   Psalm 39:12


   Psalm 42:3


3. How did Hezekiah weep?


4. Explain the situations in which the following people wept.

   **Hagar** in Genesis 21:14-16:


   **David** and **Jonathan;** scan all of 1 Samuel 20 (read verses 41-42):


   **Peter** in Matthew 26:75:


   **Mary, the Jews,** and **Jesus** in John 11:32-35:


5. Does God notice our tears? Record Psalm 56:8 from *The Living Bible*, if one is available.


6. What is God's promise to us about our tears? Summarize below.

   Isaiah 25:8


   Revelation 7:17

Hezekiah was a man of prayer. When things were going well he prayed, and when he was sick he prayed. He prayed when peaceful, and he prayed when troubled. But this prayer, after a diagnosis at age 39 of "terminal," was a heart-wrenching prayer of agony. He cried with bitterness of his soul, knowing that his life was to be so short and that he would die without an heir. He didn't demand that God heal him but tearfully pled for God to remember and deliver him.

Tears represented the agony of Hezekiah's soul. *Guideposts Family Concordance* defines tears as "drops of salty water that moisten and clean the eyes." Tears keep our eyes healthy by cleaning foreign particles like dust and hair from the cornea. The lacrimal fluid contains substances that fight bacteria and proteins that help make the eye immune to infection. If we did not have tears, our eyes would dry out and we would go blind.

Tears also moisten the soul to honestly plead before God, and they cleanse the heart of its pain. Don't we often feel better after a good cry as if all the tension has been cleared away? Don't our tears show our sensitivity to our own feelings and those of others? This protects us from spiritual blindness. Tears of agony taken to God in prayer bring healing.

Tears that come too often may indicate depression. But tears that happen in a painful event are healthful to express. Hopefully they lead us to prayer. As we present these tears to God, He takes each one of them and stores them in a bottle. He writes a record of them, for He is acutely aware of our pain. A wonderful counseling technique for someone in pain is to give him or her a visual picture of God taking each one of his or her tears and putting it in a bottle. We have no way of knowing how big this bottle is. But if the person will continue to express his or her pain to God, when the bottle is full, he or she will be healed of that grief.

Hezekiah was fortunate that his tears and prayer brought physical healing. While crying helps us feel better, God may not intervene in our situation and bring about a miracle. So if you ask God to remember and deliver, but you're not delivered, remember these points. First, your sins are still forgiven. Second, His grace is sufficient to face any difficulty. Third, our goal is not to have a smooth ride but to reach heaven. Not all tears have a powerful result, but God will use your tears to your benefit.

Lions may not cry, but what does the scripture say could happen to them?

# Ten Steps

**Read Isaiah 38:4-8; 38:21-22.**

1. List the chronological order of how these events in to-day's scripture occurred, which are better told in 2 Kings 20:4-11.

2. Read and summarize another story of God controlling the sun: Joshua 10:7-14.

3. Let's look at the two actions Hezekiah took in order to give God opportunity for a miracle. Applying the poultice was one. State the other action found in Isaiah 38:2.

4. Other stories in the Bible show a step someone had to take for God to work. Tell each person's step in the following passages.

   2 Kings 5:1-2 and 8-14

   Luke 5:1-6

   John 2:1-9

5. When God was teaching me that I had a part to play in His plan unfolding in my life, He sent me to Psalm 85:8. From this scripture, list two actions the psalmist was to take and the action God would take.

What God says, He will do. Jehovah is the undisputed Master of the universe, and no one can change that truth. Often when God wants to work one of His miracles, however, He requires us to participate. For God to take a step,

He waits for us to take a step of obedience. Hezekiah was told to prepare a poultice of figs and apply it to the boil. What if he had not bothered to do this? Naaman was angry he was asked to dip in the dirty, ugly waters of the Jordan to be healed. But unless he did his part, God would not act. The servants had to fill the jugs with water as Jesus told them, the disciples had to cast their nets once again to catch the fish, the woman with the issue of blood had to touch the hem of Jesus' garment, Peter had to go catch the fish to get the gold coin out of its mouth for the taxes, and the paraplegic had to be willing to let his friends lower him through the roof to Jesus. We often have a part in our own miracles, whether big or small, that God provides in our lives.

Through Psalm 85 God taught me that my part was to listen to what He told me to do and then not return to my old actions. If He told me to love an unlovable person in my life no matter what, I was not to forget about that in a year and return to treating him or her without love. If He told me to no longer read a certain author I enjoyed, I was not to give it up for a couple of years and then return to my folly. I had a part to play. If I played my part, God promised me peace. He would fulfill His promise if I obeyed.

Often we don't have to take 10 steps—but just 1—1 step of obedience for God to unleash His plan in our lives. Do you have a step you need to take today?

What would your list of "good things" be? Write them here.

## DAY FOUR

# Testimony

**Read Isaiah 38:9-20.**

1. Summarize the first section of Hezekiah's poem found in verses 10-14.

2. Have you ever felt the despair Hezekiah experienced as described in the above verses? Summarize other Bible characters' distress that was similar.

   Psalm 57:1-2, 4

   Psalm 60:1-3

   Psalm 77:7-9

3. The second section of Hezekiah's poem turns to thanksgiving for deliverance. Summarize Isaiah 38:15-20.

4. The psalmist David also gave praise in his distress. Summarize the following scriptures.

   Psalm 59:16-17

   Psalm 61:3-5

   Psalm 63:3-4

5. The reason God delivered Hezekiah is possibly found in Psalm 18:19. Record it here.

6. Some commentators believe Hezekiah may have written Psalm 116 after his recovery. It's a beautiful psalm of deliverance. Pick out five to ten phrases that are meaningful to you, and write them below.

For many of us who grew up in the church, Wednesday night was the time for prayer meeting and testimony service. The congregation would come together for an hour to sing, pray, and praise the Lord through personal testimonies of how God was working in their lives. I can remember some old saints in my church who would get up on a regular basis just to praise the Lord for His goodness and love. I was especially spellbound if one of my parents got up to speak. These stories had great value for passing from one generation to the next the workings of God in our lives.

In Wisdom of the Word we follow the same idea with our sharing time. We're excited to hear people tell of a current happening in their lives in which their trust in God increased or they learned more of Him. Praise is the result.

Hezekiah penned this poem after his recovery. It gives his thoughts when he was sick and his thanksgiving when he got well. Notice that when he was sick his thoughts were mainly of himself. This is a great temptation when we're in a crisis situation. Yet Hezekiah's trust remained in Yahweh even before his deliverance. He recalls his illness and how hope was dim. He tells of the plight of the sufferer. But then he gives praise to God for deliverance. This poem is Hezekiah's testimony.

As Christians we each have a testimony. It may not be flashy or exciting, but it doesn't have to be, for God's working in our lives is always powerful. Just His presence and hand in our lives are flashy enough. As I studied this lesson, I found a notation in my Bible from Psalm 116:8-9 dated 2-28-94, marked "my testimony"—*For you, O LORD, have delivered my soul from death, my eyes from tears, my feet from stumbling, that I may walk before the LORD in the land of the living.*

Each of us has a story of accepting Christ as our Savior. If we do our best to walk with God, then we have big and little happenings in our lives in which we see God at work. For example, recently my 14-year-old son, Daniel, and I were going home from a trip and trying to return our rental car. They had given us wrong directions to our motel when we originally left the rental car dealer, so in a strange place we were trying to follow incorrect directions backward. Ask anyone in my family if I'm good at directions, and the answer will be an emphatic "no." I knew I needed God's help, and I was praying out loud. I stopped at a convenience store to ask for help. The girl's directions did not fit the other directions, so my distress became greater. I didn't know what to do. But as I continued to plead for Jesus' help (so we wouldn't miss our plane), I decided to follow the girl's directions. They took us straight to our rental car dealer. Daniel and I thanked and praised the Lord profusely.

To me, that's a testimony. Was it small? Yes, as far as the important things of life go. But it was God working in our lives. He was gracious and led us—and that is reason to tell that story to others. It points to the goodness of God.

You have a testimony of salvation. Do you have current events to tell of God's goodness? Look for them in your life, and share them with others.

## MEMORY CHALLENGE

What do those who seek the Lord lack?

# Treasures

**Read Isaiah 39, concentrating on verses 1-4.**

1. What was sent to Hezekiah, by whom and why?

2. What was Hezekiah's response to this envoy?

3. Summarize 2 Chronicles 32:27-29, which gives a more detailed description of Hezekiah's wealth.

4. What did Hezekiah withhold from showing the envoy?

5. Hezekiah was unwise to show all his treasures to strangers. In 2 Chronicles 32:25 find the answer to why he did this.

6. Summarize the following warnings in Proverbs against pride.

   Proverbs 11:2

   Proverbs 16:18

   Proverbs 26:12

   Proverbs 29:23

Remember that chronologically Isaiah 38 and 39 occurred before Isaiah 36 and 37. So Hezekiah's illness, death sentence, weeping, and healing all took place before the deliverance of Jerusalem. The threat of Assyria had not come yet, and Hezekiah was on a high due to his healing. We are often at our most vulnerable after a spiritual mountaintop experience. Humanly, we begin to think that God is blessing us and that we're safe from all threats. Just when we should be on the alert, spiritually we may be asleep.

Hezekiah fell prey to this. When the envoy came from Babylon, that nation was no more than a struggling city on the banks of the Euphrates River. Certainly they were no renowned world power. Hezekiah learned of their strength from Isaiah's prophecy after showing them the national treasures.

This envoy had a threefold purpose. The first was to congratulate Hezekiah on his miraculous recovery. The second was to hopefully form an alliance against Assyria with Judah. Remember—this was something at which Isaiah kept hammering—no foreign alliance. But the Babylonians hated the Assyrians and wanted to be friends with anyone who would stand against them. The third purpose of the envoy was the performance of their god. The Babylonians worshiped the sun. They thought Hezekiah must be very special if their sun would go back 10 steps for him.

So the *foot of pride* (Psalm 36:11) came upon Hezekiah. It started with flattering letters and a gift and ended with the revealing of national secrets. Babylon didn't need spies— Hezekiah told all.

Have you ever trusted the wrong person out of pride? Maybe he or she played up to you and rejoiced with you just like the Babylonian envoy. Most of us would think this was wonderful and that we had found a friend. Does the pride of someone liking us sometimes take away our discernment? The person likes us, so we in turn try to impress him or her.

Hezekiah's treasures were of silver, gold, spices, and oil, but our treasures may not be material. They may be confidences or children or relationships or messages from God. We need to be careful with whom we trust our treasures. Pride encourages us to show them off. Wisdom encourages us to use discernment.

Isaiah confronts Hezekiah, and he confesses. The allure of these treasures possibly faded in Hezekiah's eyes, for when Assyria laid seige to Jerusalem the first time, these were the items Hezekiah sent them as a peace offering (2 Kings 18:13-16). Hezekiah was a godly king who learned from his sins. He realized pride had won, and he had looked for a stamp of approval from people instead of from God. As he turned from his pride, Hezekiah found his true treasure—His relationship with the Lord. Does your pride stand between you and God? Have you become focused on your treasures instead of the true Treasure? If so, this is the moment of opportunity today to make a change. Pray about it now.

## MEMORY CHALLENGE

Fill in the blanks:

*The _____ may grow weak and _____, but those who _____ the _____ lack no _____ thing.*

Psalm 34:10

## DAY SIX

# Trade for Peace

**Read Isaiah 39:5-8.**

1. What did Isaiah tell Hezekiah was the consequence of showing his treasure to the Babylonians?

2. What was Hezekiah's response?

3. What are your thoughts about Hezekiah's response?

4. Where does true peace come from? Summarize the following scriptures.

   Isaiah 26:12

   Jeremiah 33:6

5. Summarize the following passages, which explain how our peace relates to our relationship with Jesus Christ.

   Isaiah 53:5

   Romans 5:1

   Colossians 1:20

6. Record the following scriptures, which tell us to pursue peace.

   Psalm 34:14

   2 Timothy 2:22

7. If we are to pursue peace, what does Christ mean in Matthew 10:34?

Hezekiah's pride is brought down by a humbling message. He is told that he acted like a foolish traveler who shows his money and gold to a man who is a thief. Imagine how irritated he could have been at himself at first notice. You know the feeling when you have said too much, boasted or shown off to the wrong person, but it's too late to take it back. That sinking feeling creeps in.

But Hezekiah quickly responds, *The word of the LORD you have spoken is good.* He thought, *There will be peace and security in my lifetime* (Isaiah 39:8). Either he is good at accepting his punishment or grateful he will not suffer the consequences. Either Hezekiah has the acceptance of a mature adult or the relief of an immature person. Maybe hearing of a descendant was a possible reason for him to be cheerful, for remember: Hezekiah had no heir at the time he fell ill.

However, some commentators believe that it's possible Hezekiah wanted peace in his lifetime whatever the cost. If this is so, it is a dangerous philosophy.

God is the one who establishes peace for us. Psalm 29:11 tells us that peace is a blessing. As Christians, we're given peace through Christ's blood and sacrifice on the Cross. So peace is God's blessing to us as we keep our relationship with Christ pure. Peace is not in our circumstances or in our power to grasp.

When we are told to seek peace, it means that we are to seek peace with God by keeping our lives free from sin. Our relationship with God is our source of peace. When Christ said He came to bring a sword, not peace, He was referring to choosing to follow God. Whatever that takes, we are to do it whether it disturbs our circumstantial peace or not.

We are into peace in our culture. We want no discomfort to our life circumstances. However, sometimes following Christ means there is no peace. When I choose to discipline my children and they are mad about it, I am not choosing peace, but I *am* choosing what's right. The modern-day version of "This hurts me more than it does you" is that the parents suffer more than their teenager when the teenager is grounded. But if the teenager needs to be disciplined, that's what's right. To choose peace and let the teenager off the hook is way too common to our way of thinking. This may bring a temporary peace, but in the long run it brings tragedy.

We must live our lives for the big picture of eternity. To choose peace when a sword is needed is living life for the moment of comfort.

Maybe Hezekiah had that modern-day attitude of "What do I care? I won't be here to worry about it." He was happy for peace in his lifetime. Was he willing to trade peace for what was right? We don't know for sure about Hezekiah, but it's a good question to ask ourselves. Do we trade what is right for peace? Peace at all costs is too high a price to pay. If this is a problem in your life, take time now to let the Holy Spirit talk with you about it. Then make a commitment to Him about it.

*Written by Linda Shaw*

## MEMORY CHALLENGE

Write out this week's memory verse.

# Notes

## Introduction to Isaiah
1. *Beacon Bible Commentary*, vol. 4, *Isaiah Through Daniel*, ed. Ross E. Price (Kansas City: Beacon Hill Press of Kansas City, 1966), 48.

## Lesson 1, Day 2
1. J. Vernon McGee, *Isaiah, Chapters 1-35* (Nashville: Thomas Nelson Publishers, 1991), 27.

## Lesson 1, Day 3
1. W. E. Vine, *Vine's Expository Commentary on Isaiah* (Nashville: Thomas Nelson Publishers, 1997), 9.

## Lesson 1, Day 5
1. Charles Colson, *Born Again* (Old Tappan, N.J.: Chosen Books, 1972), 11.
2. Ibid., 21.
3. Ibid., 22.
4. Ibid., 9.

## Lesson 1, Day 6
1. J. I. Packer, Merrill C. Tenney, and William White Jr., *The Bible Almanac* (Carmel, N.Y.: Guideposts, Thomas Nelson Publishers, 1980), 503.

## Lesson 2, Day 1
1. *Beacon Bible Commentary, Isaiah Through Daniel*, 44-45.

## Lesson 2, Day 4
1. *Vine's Expository Commentary on Isaiah*, 23.

## Lesson 2, Day 5
1. *Beacon Bible Commentary, Isaiah Through Daniel*, 52.
2. Ibid.

## Lesson 3, Day 1
1. *Vine's Expository Commentary on Isaiah*, 25.

## Lesson 3, Day 2
1. David McKenna, *Mastering the Old Testament, Isaiah 1—39* (Dallas: Word Publishing, 1993), 131.
2. Bruce M. Metzger and Michael D. Coogan, eds., *The Oxford Companion to the Bible* (New York: Oxford University Press, 1993), 300.

## Lesson 3, Day 3
1. "The Antiquities of the Jews," *The Works of Flavius Josephus*, complete and unabridged new revised edition, tran. William Whiston (Peabody, Mass.: Hendrickson Publishers, 1987), 262-63.
2. *Vine's Expository Commentary on Isaiah*, 27.
3. Larry Richards, *Every Covenant and Every Promise in the Bible* (Nashville: Thomas Nelson Publishers, 1998), 140.

## Lesson 3, Day 4
1. McKenna, *Mastering the Old Testament, Isaiah 1—39*, 135.

## Lesson 3, Day 5
1. J. Vernon McGee, *Through the Bible Commentary Series* (Nashville: Thomas Nelson Publishers, 1991), 22:90.

## Lesson 3, Day 6
1. *Beacon Bible Commentary*, vol. 6, *Matthew, Mark, Luke*, ed. Ralph Earle (Kansas City: Beacon Hill Press, 1964), 2-64.

## Lesson 4, Day 2
1. *The Complete Bible Commentary* (Nashville: Thomas Nelson Publishers, 1999; Old-Time Gospel Hour, 1983), 785.
2. *Beacon Bible Commentary, Isaiah Through Daniel*, 66.
3. Geoffrey W. Grogan, *Zondervan NIV Bible Commentary* (Grand Rapids: Zondervan Publishing House, 1994), 1:1062.

4. *Life Application Bible, New International Version* (Wheaton, Ill.: Tyndale House Publishers; and Grand Rapids: Zondervan Publishing House, 1991), 118.

## Lesson 4, Day 4
1. McGee, *Through the Bible Commentary Series*, 22:109.

## Lesson 4, Day 5
1. *Life Application Bible*, 1226.

## Lesson 6, Day 3
1. *Vine's Expository Commentary on Isaiah*, 57.

## Lesson 6, Day 4
1. "A Conversation with Frank Minirth," *Christian Counseling Today*, 8:3 (August 2000), 41-43.

## Lesson 7, Day 1
1. Matthew Black, gen. ed., and H. H. Rowley, Old Testament ed., *Peake's Commentary on the Bible* (Nairobi, Kenya: Thomas Nelson Publishers, 1962), 508.
2. McGee, *Isaiah, Chapters 1-35*, 192.

## Lesson 7, Day 2
1. *Peake's Commentary on the Bible*, 508.

## Lesson 8, Day 2
1. *Beacon Bible Commentary, Isaiah Through Daniel*, 138.

## Lesson 8, Day 3
1. *NIV Life Application Bible*, 2240.
2. Ibid., 2279.
3. *Beacon Bible Commentary, Isaiah Through Daniel*, 140.

## Lesson 8, Day 4
1. Walter Elwell, ed., *Evangelical Commentary on the Bible*, 497. [NEED FULL PUBLICATION DATA]
2. Kenneth Barker and John Kohlenberger III, eds., *NIV Bible Commentary, Vol. 1: Old Testament* (Grand Rapids: Zondervan Publishing House, 1994), 1107.

## Lesson 8, Day 5
1. Josh McDowell and Don Stewart, *Answers to Tough Questions* (San Bernardino, Calif.: Here's Life Publishers, 1980), 69.
2. Metzger and Coogan, *Oxford Companion to the Bible*, 788.
3. McDowell and Stewart, *Answers to Tough Questions*, 69.
4. Ibid., 70.
5. Metzger and Coogan, *Oxford Companion to the Bible*, 788.

## Lesson 8, Day 6
1. David McKenna, *Mastering the Old Testament*, 329.
2. Quoted in *Beacon Bible Commentary, Isaiah Through Daniel*, 148

## Lesson 9, Day 5
1. *Beacon Bible Commentary, Isaiah—Daniel*, 150.
2. William J. Murray, *My Life Without God* (Nashville: Thomas Nelson Publishers, 1982), 14.
3. Ibid., 246.
4. Ibid., 245.

## Lesson 10, Day 1
1. Betty Rollin, *First You Cry* [FULL PUBLICATION DATA NEEDED].
2. *Matthew Henry's Commentary* [FULL PUBLICATION DATA NEEDED], 880.
3. [QUOTE FROM EDDIE SUTTON—TITLE AND FULL PUBLICATION DATA NEEDED]